Sweet Comfort for the Ailing Saint

Ebenezer Nyarko

These were more noble than those in Thessalonica, in that they received the word with all readiness of mind, and searched the scriptures daily, whether those things were so (Acts 17:11).

ISBN: 978-9988-2-7903-5

Designed by Dela Anyah

Table of Contents

Chapter 1 : Where does sickness come from?

God is in every way opposed to the devil. In Genesis 3.15, He declared war against him - Christ against the devil and the devil against Christ. Of course, the devil is no match for Christ. The remarkable victory against satan was gained at the cross of Calvary, disarming and disgracing the evil one and his principalities and powers, thereby rendering them impotent (Colossians 2.15). The devil, however, always tries to regain his former position of authority, which he lost when he was cast out of Heaven. He also tries to torment Christians still, since he is opposed to Christ and his body – the church.

The main reason is the fact that he has a short time to remain upon the earth until he and his demons are permanently done away with (Revelation 12.12, Matthew 25.41). Not only is the devil the father of sin (1 John 3.8), but he is also the cause of many sicknesses and diseases. Jesus came to the earth to heal these sicknesses and diseases because He knew that those that had them were being oppressed by the devil - "how

God anointed Jesus of Nazareth with the Holy Spirit and with power, who went about doing good and healing all who were oppressed by the devil, for God was with Him" (Acts 10:38). The Bible refers to sickness as satanic oppression and thank God that Jesus is here to deliver us from his evil schemes. "So ought not this woman, being a daughter of Abraham, whom Satan has bound-- think of it-- for eighteen years, be loosed from this bond on the Sabbath?" (Luke 13:16).

 The main work of the devil is to steal, to kill and to destroy. On the other hand, the primary mission of Jesus is to bring us abundant life (John 10.10). The work of the devil and the work of Christ are thus, at opposite ends; the one wants to bring destruction – the other, abundant life. If you are sick, be of good cheer, "for this purpose the Son of God was manifested, that he might destroy the works of the devil" (1 John 3:8). The devil is the father of sin and Jesus came to release us from his bondages, which primarily consist of sin and sickness. The devil oppresses and Jesus brings liberty. Jesus came to destroy the works of the devil (1 John 3.8). Sin and sicknesses are works of the devil and God wants to free you from them. The reason God sent Jesus into the earth was to liberate you from the oppression of the wicked one. We, therefore, have to stand against sickness and disease in the same way that we stand against sin and the devil. The Bible exhorts us not to "give place to the devil" ((Ephesians 4.27). As a result, if we are not giving place to the devil then consequently, we must not give place to his works as well, which include sickness and disease.

Even in the Old Testament, we find that God was willing to heal the sicknesses and diseases of His Covenant people, not wanting to permit the enemy to afflict them with sicknesses if they obeyed Him. "If you diligently heed the voice of the LORD your God and do what is right in His sight, give ear to His commandments and keep all His statutes, I will put none of the diseases on you which I have brought on the Egyptians. For I am the LORD who heals you" (Exodus 15:26). In the Bible, Egypt usually symbolizes the world and thus, God was letting them know that if they heeded to His statutes, He would not allow the god of this world, satan, to afflict them with illnesses in the way in which he was afflicting the people of the world. "So you shall serve the LORD your God, and He will bless your bread and your water. And I will take sickness away from the midst of you. No one shall suffer miscarriage or be barren in your land; I will fulfill the number of your days" (Exodus 23:25-26). The God of love was letting them know that if they served Him, He would also bless them and take sicknesses and diseases away from them. When the Israelites, kept the covenant, God was also faithful and didn't allow any sicknesses to prevail amongst them just as he had told them previously, because He does not lie and fulfills everything that He says (Numbers 23.19).

Furthermore, in the Book of Deuteronomy, God lets the Israelites know that He would bless them abundantly and would take away their illnesses. "Then it shall come to pass, because you listen to these judgments, and keep and do them, that the LORD your God will keep with you the covenant and the mercy which He swore to your fathers............You shall be blessed above all peoples; there shall not be a male or female barren among you or among your livestock. And the LORD will take away from you all sickness, and will afflict you with none of the terrible diseases of Egypt which you have known, but will lay them on all those who hate you" (Deuteronomy 7:12,14-15). The Lord was reminding them that if they kept His Covenant of mercy and were obedient, He would bless them greatly and would take away all sicknesses and diseases from their midst. The devil is a deceiver, but God is a healer.

There is a close connection between sin and sickness. First and foremost, both come from the devil. The devil likes to bring separation between God and man - he also wants to oppress man with sickness. Sickness, sin and death came into the world when Adam was tempted in the Garden of Eden and fell from grace. As the Bible tells us, "wherefore, as by one man sin entered into the world, and death by sin; and so death passed upon all men, for that all have sinned" (Romans 5.12). But God did not stop there – even before He created the world, He had made provision for man's sin and sickness (Revelation 13.8). As a result, He came to die on the cross of Calvary as the second Adam to release humankind from the bondage he had been plunged into due to Adam's first sin - "but God demonstrates His own love toward us, in that while we were still sinners, Christ died for us" (Romans 5.8). Though sickness, sin and death had come from the devil and have been passed through Adam to the whole of humanity, God would send His only begotten Son as a gift to restore abundant life, health and righteousness. "For if by the one man's offense many died, much more the grace of God and the gift by the grace of the one Man, Jesus Christ, abounded to many. And the gift is not like that which came through the one who sinned. For the judgment which came from one offense resulted in condemnation, but the free gift which came from many offenses resulted in justification. For if by the one man's offense death reigned through the one, much more those who receive abundance of grace and of the gift of righteousness will reign in life through the One, Jesus Christ" (Romans 5.15-17).

Yes, sin and sickness came from Adam's first sin. The spirit and soul had been afflicted by sin and the body, by sickness. When Jesus came, He brought along with him forgiveness for the soul and spirit, as well as, healing for the body. All three aspects of man - his spirit, soul and body are important to Him (1 Thessalonians 5.23). Jesus started His ministry on earth healing sicknesses and diseases and ended it by becoming a propitiation for man's sin on the cross. Sin and sickness come from the devil; forgiveness and healing come from Jesus Christ. He saves us from sins and sicknesses because both are an essential part of the salvation He gained for us on the cross (Psalm 103.3, Isaiah 53.4-5). Jesus shows His love for you and me by forgiving our sins and healing our sicknesses. The Greek word for salvation is 'soteria.' The Strong's Greek Concordance defines it as 'welfare, prosperity, deliverance, preservation, salvation, safety.' So as you can see, salvation does not just point to the salvation of your soul only but also your total welfare and prosperity, including the deliverance of your body from sickness. You thought it was just the salvation of your soul – no, it's a comprehensive package. Sometimes Jesus forgave people and then healed their diseases. At other times He healed their diseases and then forgave their sins.

In the Bible, we see that of all the recorded works of Jesus, most of them involved healings. Apart from salvation, one of the greatest blessings is healing. "He said to him, 'man, your sins are forgiven you............'But that you may know that the Son of Man has power on earth to forgive sins' (He said to the man who was paralyzed), 'I say to you, arise, take up your bed, and go to your house'" (Luke 5:20, 24). In this case, Jesus let the man know that His sins had been forgiven before healing Him. After His sins were forgiven, He didn't want the man to remain disease-stricken in his bed but healed him as well. Some people think that sin is a spiritual issue that God dislikes and that sickness is a bodily affliction, which He is not concerned with. God, however, sees sin and sickness as coming from the devil and that is exactly why He came, "that He might destroy the works of the devil" (1 John 3:8).

A school of thought teaches that some sicknesses of believers are due to the chastening of the Lord. For example, in the case of Miriam, Moses' sister, who was struck with leprosy due to her complaints against Moses (Numbers 12.1-15). Seven main sins can be detected; firstly, the sin of rebellion and wrongful criticism, where Miriam and Aaron castigated Moses for his marriage to Zipporah, the Cushite. They were actually rebelling against the authority of Moses, using his wife as a cover-up. Secondly, the sin of jealousy and envy where Moses consulted Jethro, his father-in-law who advised him to get seventy elders that would help him in his task of overseeing the Israelites. Miriam was not included among these seventy; her criticism of Moses was a cover-up of their jealousy. Thirdly, Miriam was being racially prejudiced when she complained about the race of Moses' wife Zipporah. Miriam and Aaron were envious and unhappy that they had gone to his wife's father for advice instead of consulting them. Fourthly, Miriam was guilty of spiritual pride when she complained that Moses was not the only person that God spoke to and that God spoke to her as well since she was a prophetess. The fact that she was a spiritually gifted prophetess did not mean that she had the right to challenge God's authority on how His people should be managed. Also, Miriam was guilty of selfishness - "let nothing be done through selfish ambition or conceit, but in lowliness of mind let each esteem others better than himself" (Philippians 2:3). She should have been happy that a solution had come up for the administration of Israel, but she thought that she should have been placed at the helm of affairs. Miriam was also guilty of the sin of hatred. Her jealousy, envy, criticism, racial prejudice, selfishness and pride had now graduated to hatred - the complete opposite of love. "But he who hates his brother is in darkness and walks in darkness, and does not know where he is going, because the darkness has blinded his eyes" (1st John 2:11). Finally, Miriam and Aaron saw that they were being foolish in their complaints against Moses. "So Aaron said to Moses, 'oh, my Lord! Please do not lay this sin on us, in which we have done foolishly and in which we have sinned" (Numbers 12.11). God had struck her with leprosy and consequently, she needed to confess it in order to receive healing. Moses had not made any defense of himself, it was God who defended Him. The Bible tells us that, "Moses was very humble, more than all men who were on the face of the earth" (Numbers 12:3). Moses interceded for Miriam and though the Lord let her retain her leprous condition for seven days, being shut out of the camp, God healed her afterwards. Psalm 107.11-20 gives us a certain progression of healing which can be applied to Miriam's case. She began with self-sufficiency - to disaster - to repentance - to deliverance and then finally thanksgiving. At first she was self-sufficient leading to her disease. She then repented and was delivered. Now she had every reason to thank God. This progression is also similar to the sequence of events that occur when one is getting saved; conviction of sin – faith – repentance - salvation, and grateful worship.

If you are a believer and you think you have an affliction, which indeed is from God, you can be encouraged by Miriam's healing after her chastening since confession and repentance would lead to healing (1 John 1.8-9, James 5.16). Repentance is 'metanoeo' in the Greek, which means change of mind or direction. If a believer feels his sickness is as a result of being chastened of God, "for whom the Lord loves He chastens" (Hebrews 12.6), he should be at ease and realize he that if he changes his mind and turns to God, He is more than willing to receive him. In the case of the paralytic, "when Jesus saw their faith, He said to the paralytic, 'Son, your sins are forgiven you............but that you may know that the Son of Man has power on earth to forgive sins'.............'I say to you, arise, take up your bed, and go to your house" (Mark 2.5,10-11).

Leprosy as a type of sin

In the Bible, leprosy is a type of sin or speaks of sin and its destructive ability. Before we consider the spiritual connotations of leprosy, it would also be important to look at the physical nature of the disease. Though it shows on the skin, it goes in deeper than the skin's surface (Leviticus 13.3). It has the ability to spread

(Leviticus 13.5-8). Furthermore, it has the ability to defile and isolate (Leviticus 13.44-46). These features are very similar to the effects of sin. Moreover, it is an infectious disease, which causes skin sores, nerve damage and progressive dehabilitation. Some of its symptoms include skin lesions lighter than the normal skin colour that have decreased sensation to touch, heat or pain. These lesions also take a long time to heal, taking up to several weeks and months. Another symptom is numbness in the limbs. The word 'leprosy,' also known as 'Hansen's disease', is caused by an organism known as mycobacterium leprae. Though it is not easily contagious, it however, has a long incubation period that makes it hard to pinpoint when the ailment was actually contracted. The infection leads to peripheral neurological damage that leads to sensory loss in the skin, as well as muscle weakness. The long-term leprosy causes the loss of the ability to use the hands and feet due to a loss of sensation in those areas of the afflicted individual.

Leviticus 13 contains many instructions that show how to deal with leprosy, as well as other skin infections. The person suspected with the disease had to go to the priest to be examined and had to dress in an odd manner. He also had to go through town shouting the words, 'unclean, unclean'- he was seen to be unclean and had to live alone, isolated from the rest of the camp. This was supposed to point to his uncleanness, physically and spiritually. He wasn't allowed to come within six feet of anyone else, including his own family members and also wasn't allowed to come within 150 feet of anyone when the wind was blowing. They only lived with other lepers until their condition improved or until they passed away, which was how the disease was controlled, so it wouldn't spread to anyone else. Leprosy was incurable by man.

When Jesus came He, however, healed leprosy (or sin) - a reproach that defiled man in God's eyes. It is Christ who is the mediator, redeemer and healer of the sin condition and the sickness that it brings. God abhors sin and finds it very repulsive. As a result, it prevents Him from accepting the sinner into His presence (Revelation 21.27, Habakkuk 1.13, Psalm 5.5). Christ has, however, made provision so we can be redeemed by His atoning work on the Cross and through the shedding of His precious blood. All those who believe in His death and resurrection and know Him as their Lord and personal Saviour are justified before God, giving them the ability to stand in His presence. When Simon Peter saw the goodness of God, he said, "depart from me; for I am a sinful man, O Lord" (Luke 5:8). When Isaiah came to terms with the Holiness of God, he said, "woe is me! For I am undone; because I am a man of unclean lips, and I dwell in the midst of a people of unclean lips: for mine eyes have seen the King, the LORD of hosts" (Isaiah 6:5). Through Jesus Christ, we can be washed in His blood and with His Word (1st Corinthians 6.11, Ephesians 5.26, 1 John 1.7). His Word tells us, "having predestinated us unto the adoption of children by Jesus Christ to himself, according to the good pleasure of his will, to the praise of the glory of his grace, wherein he hath made us accepted in the beloved" (Ephesians 1:5-6). Because of the abundant grace that is in Him, let us come to Him for forgiveness, because He will not cast anyone away (John 6.37, Hebrews 4.16, Psalm 103.12).

Chapter 2: A Clean 'bill of health' paid for on the Cross

Sin and sickness were introduced into the world through the devil and the event of the temptation of Adam, causing him to fall from grace. The consequences of this fall affected all of humanity (Romans 5.12). The good news is, Jesus Christ is, however, our Redeemer from sin and sickness (Isaiah 53.4-5, Colossians 1.13-14, Galatians 3.13-14). It was very costly when the devil gave sin and sickness the opportunity to enter the world. It was a very hefty price - a huge expense to all humanity. But through Jesus, we can and have received the ability to be free from both the power of sin and the sickness that it brings. "For if by the one man's offense death reigned through the one, much more those who receive abundance of grace and of the gift of righteousness will reign in life through the One, Jesus Christ" (Romans 5.17). Jesus paid for our redemption from both sin and sickness on the Cross of Calvary and obtained salvation for all who would believe. "For all have sinned and fall short of the glory of God, being justified freely by His grace through the redemption that is in Christ Jesus, whom God set forth as a propitiation by His blood, through faith" (Romans 3.23-25). Jesus paid the price for our redemption and healing with His blood on the cross (Hebrews 9.12-14, Ephesians 1.7, Matthew 26.27-28, Romans 5.9). As it were, Jesus has paid the price to release us from the evil grips of the devil who oppresses us with sin and sickness. When He said it is finished, He had gained victory over the devil and his evil works. He paid for it all with His most precious blood, shed for you and me, "the church of God which He purchased with His own blood" (Acts 20:28).

In the Bible, silver usually speaks of the redemptive blood of Jesus. When the tabernacle of Moses was being constructed, it rested on silver sockets that supported it (Exodus 38.27). This reveals to us that we obtain rest from the blood of Jesus. It is important to note that the ministry of Jesus (represented as the tabernacle) heavily dwelt upon His redemptive blood. Moreover, when Judas threw 30 pieces of silver on the floor, he said he had betrayed innocent blood (Matthew 27.3-4) further establishing the link between silver and blood. Silver is a precious coin – silver is used for payment – silver points to the redemptive blood of Jesus – Jesus paid for our redemption with His precious blood.

Exodus 30.13-16 gives us more background information on redemption. All the Israelites that were twenty years and above had to pay a half-shekel to the Lord, through the high priest. It was an individual thing and everybody had to pay their own redemption money; it was not supposed to cover groups. They all had to give an equal amount of a half-shekel; nothing more, nothing less. This was to show that everyone owed God and was obligated to Him. This amount was considered as redemption money and the Israelites would confess that they deserved to die, accepting that they were in debt to God and that the money that they were paying was a type of redemption, which would be paid for the souls of men. Eventually, this half-shekel became the amount that needed to be paid as a yearly temple tax (Matthew 17.24). The poor did not need to pay a lower amount and the rich didn't need to pay a higher amount; it was a flat rate of a half-shekel because all souls are equally precious to God. It wasn't about any special characteristics of those paying the money or any special circumstances pertaining to them; all had to pay the standard fee. The redemption was the key thing here and not any other factor. Through the sin of one man, death had passed onto all men (Romans 5.12) and it would take one fee paid by one man to redeem humanity (Romans 5.15). It served as a representation of the cost of our redemption and all who paid this money were atoned. The money taken was used in the building of the tabernacle because large amounts of silver were needed in building it. They were used for the silver sockets of the tabernacle which sustained it and since the tabernacle rested on these sockets (the silver points to the blood of Jesus), it is the blood of Jesus which sustains us.

"And I said unto them, If ye think good, give me my price; and if not, forbear. So they weighed for my price thirty pieces of silver. And the Lord said unto me, Cast it unto the potter: a goodly price that I was prised at of them. And I took the thirty pieces of silver, and cast them to the potter in the house of the Lord" (Zechariah 11.12-13).

Jesus was betrayed to the chief priests for 30 pieces of silver by Judas. Silver represents blood. When Judas cast down the silver pieces on the floor, he went and hang himself afterwards. The chief priests thought the money was not worthy of being put into the temple treasury because it was "the price of blood" (Matthew 27.6). The 'blood money' was consequently used to purchase the potter's field and that field became known as the field of blood. Similarly, the blood of Jesus is spiritual currency that can be used as spiritual legal tender to purchase back your health.

The blood of Jesus is able to overcome the devil, sin and sickness. "And they overcame him by the blood of the Lamb" (Revelation 12:11). It was a marvelous victory that Jesus gained on the cross. He put a grinding halt to the devious works of the devil and his demonic spirits, stripping them of their power (Colossians 2.15). He took our sins and sicknesses upon Himself on the cross. Some people refer to Isaiah 53 as the Gospel in the Old Testament. It tells us "surely He has borne our griefs and carried our sorrows; yet we esteemed Him stricken, smitten by God and afflicted. But He was wounded for our transgressions, He was bruised for our iniquities; the chastisement for our peace was upon Him, and by His stripes we are healed" (Isaiah 53.4-5). Griefs in the Hebrew is 'choliy', which means sicknesses in English. On the cross He carried all our sicknesses; He felt how it is to be sick; He felt our pain; He felt our infirmities. Our pain is His pain, our sicknesses have been placed upon Him and our sins also. He was fulfilling Galatians 6.2 which says, "bear one another's burdens, and so fulfill the law of Christ" (Galatians 6.2). Though He Himself did not sin, He felt the weight of it. "For we have not an high priest which cannot be touched with the feeling of our infirmities" (Hebrews 4:15). With this knowledge of the great redemption, salvation and healing He has purchased for us, we need to be grateful and "enter into His gates with thanksgiving, and into His courts with praise" (Psalm 100:4). Next, we need to receive our inheritance with faith -, "in Him we have redemption through His blood, the forgiveness of sins, according to the riches of His grace which He made to abound toward us in all wisdom and prudence............the eyes of your understanding being enlightened; that you may know what is the hope of His calling, what are the riches of the glory of His inheritance in the saints" (Ephesians 1.7-8,18). Yes, He died on the cross so we could inherit forgiveness and healing from Him. The question is, do you have the faith to appropriate these blessings?

The brazen serpent

When Moses was leading the Israelites through the wilderness, there was a time when they were making complaints to him about unfavorable conditions there. God then sent fiery serpents among the people that bit them, causing many deaths. The people approached Moses and confessed that they had sinned in complaining and that Moses should pray on their behalf so that the serpents would be taken away. Moses interceded for them and the Lord replied to Moses, saying, "make a fiery serpent, and set it on a pole; and it shall be that everyone who is bitten, when he looks at it, shall live. So Moses made a bronze serpent, and put it on a pole; and so it was, if a serpent had bitten anyone, when he looked at the bronze serpent, he lived" (Numbers 21:9-10).

The solution to the snake-bite problem was making a bronze serpent and putting it on a pole. All who looked at it would be delivered. Bronze represents judgement (Deuteronomy 28.23, Judges 16.21), the serpent represented sin, the pole was a foreshadowing of the cross. "Christ has redeemed us from the curse of the law, having become a curse for us, for it is written, 'cursed is everyone who hangs on a tree'" (Galatians 3.13). The serpent on the pole was a foreshadowing of Christ judging sin on the cross. "And as Moses lifted up the serpent in the wilderness, even so must the Son of Man be lifted up" (John 3:14). Sin and sickness come from the devil and all have been dealt with on the cross. The cross is at the heart of Christianity. It is a place of exchange - on the cross our sins, wounds and illnesses were exchanged for His. He finished it all on the cross when He said, 'it is finished' (John 19.30). Two main blessings were to be achieved by looking at the brazen serpent on the pole; spiritual blessings and physical blessings—the forgiveness of their sins and the healing of their bodies – salvation for the soul and healing for the body. They were to be forgiven for their complaints in the wilderness and then healed of the venomous bites from the serpents. The brazen serpent on the cross was to serve as a representation of what Christ was going to do on Calvary. It was supposed to point to the work, which, would be finished once-and-for-all on the cross of Calvary, not needing to be repeated anymore. Later on, in the time of Hezekiah, the brazen serpent became an idol and an object of worship. God instructed that its worship should be abolished. It's not the Cross itself that saves us but Christ and His finished work of atonement on it.

Next, we have to cast our minds to the empty tomb – because not only did He die on the cross, He also resurrected. The apostles continued preaching about the Cross and the empty tomb after His death. On the cross He was the lamb of God that took away the sins of the world, but when He resurrected, He became known as a Saviour and Redeemer. On the Cross He purchased our salvation and redemption with the blood, but when He resurrected, He went to sit on the right-hand side of God, where He intercedes for us from the mercy seat. He still lives and reigns on the throne and cares about you. "When you lift up the Son of Man, then you will know that I am He, and that I do nothing of myself; but as my Father taught Me" (John 8.28). Thank God that He sent His only begotten Son to come and help us - Alleluia. Now, there was only one thing that the people had to do; they had to look at the serpent on the cross. Who was on the cross of Calvary? Are you looking at Him and to Him for your healing? If you are, you shall be delivered and your healing will surely come.

"And as Moses lifted up the serpent in the wilderness, even so must the Son of Man be lifted up, that whoever believes in Him should not perish but have eternal life. For God so loved the world that He gave His only begotten Son, that whoever believes in Him should not perish but have everlasting life. For God did not send His Son into the world to condemn the world, but that the world through Him might be saved" (John 3.14-17). When Jesus was talking about being saved, He was talking about salvation for the body, soul and spirit. The Greek word for saved is 'sozo.' Strong's Concordance defines sozo as 'I save; heal; preserve; rescue; deliver out of danger and into safety. It is used principally of God rescuing believers from the penalty and power of sin into His provisions.' The NAS Exhaustive concordance defines it as 'bring safely; cured; ensure salvation; get; get well; made well; preserved; recover; restore; saving.'

'Sozo' is used 16 times in the New Testament to mean bodily healing in the following passages: Matthew 9:21, 22; Mark 5:23, 28, 34; 6:56; 10:52; Luke 7:50; 8:36, 48, 50; 17:19; 18:42; Acts 4:9; 14:9; James 5:15.

We often hear the term, 'the Gospel,' but what really is the Gospel? The Strong's concordance defines the term, 'gospel,' which is 'euangelion' in the Greek as the good news of the coming of the Messiah. The main subject of the Gospel is a person – the person of Jesus Christ. The Anglo-Saxon rendition of the word is 'godspell' which means good story, Good News or the glad tidings concerning salvation and the kingdom of God as announced to the world by Christ. The salvation offered by Jesus is a total package that includes your preservation, deliverance, prosperity and health. Jesus cares and knows that without your health you cannot find wholeness and fulfillment in life. Naaman for example was a very great and honorable military general, but he had an issue – he had leprosy and it made his life less than fulfilling. Eventually God granted him his healing. God wants to do the same for you. You are the reason why He left His throne in Heaven to come to the earth to die on the cross. He suffered all that agony in the Garden of Gethsemane, to go on the cross just for you. Before He was crucified he was flogged and beaten, given many stripes and bruises on His body. He took your place on the cross and became the propitiation for your sin. You are the apple of His eye and He wants to heal YOU.

"For this purpose the Son of God was manifested, that he might destroy the works of the devil" (1 John 3:8). Through the death and resurrection of Jesus on the cross, He has provided salvation and healing. In fact, He began His work of healing before going to the cross as healing was one of the main aspects of His earthly ministry, "he received them and spoke to them about the kingdom of God, and healed those who had need of healing" (Luke 9:11). One of the names of Jesus is Yahweh-Rapha, which means, "the Lord our Healer." God is revealing one aspect of His nature, the aspect of a Healer and indeed, He is a faithful God who wants to heal You. Not only was He a compassionate healer Himself, but He also gave his disciples the ability to heal. Eventually, He gave all believers the ability to heal, "and these signs shall follow them that believe; in my name shall they cast out devils............they shall lay hands on the sick, and they shall recover" (Mark 16:17-18). James lets us know that if any are sick in the church, they have the privilege of praying or calling upon the elders to come to them and pray for healing (James 5.13-15). Prayer for healing, however, requires faith on your part. God rejoices in our healing. "Beloved, I wish above all things that thou mayest prosper and be in health, even as thy soul prospereth" (3 John 1:2).

"Who his own self bare our sins in his own body on the tree, that we, being dead to sins, should live unto righteousness: by whose stripes ye were healed" (1 Peter 2.24).

Yes, you were healed when Jesus hang on the cross over 2000 years ago; it's time to enter His gates with thanksgiving (Psalm 100.4) and exercise the faith to receive that healing now. Moreover, even before the foundation of the world, God foresaw the fall, misery and predicaments that would befall man. He therefore, made arrangements with Christ to establish an atonement for his dire condition by letting His only begotten Son come and die on the Cross for us, to make atonement for all who would believe. In Genesis 3, God declared war on satan, saying, "and I will put enmity between thee and the woman, and between thy seed and her seed; it shall bruise thy head, and thou shalt bruise his heel" (Genesis 3.15). On the cross, Jesus' heel was indeed bruised as He hang on it and died there; satan's head was bruised because Christ has attained the victory against him. The atoning work on the cross was the exact reason Jesus came to the earth. "For this purpose the Son of God was manifested, that he might destroy the works of the devil" (1 John 3.8). When Peter says 'we being dead to sins,' he makes us know that because of Christ's work on the cross, we can be new creations in Him, as repentance has been made possible. "Therefore if any man be in Christ, he is a new creature: old things are passed away; behold, all things are become new" (2 Corinthians 5.17). We can also have the righteousness that is in Christ imputed into us. "For the life of the flesh is in the blood: and I have given it to you upon the altar to make an atonement for your souls: for it is the blood that maketh an atonement for the soul" (Leviticus 17.11).

His victory on the cross has many dimensions to it; it not only includes salvation for us, but also healing from our sicknesses. The blood of Jesus has brought us salvation, justification, cleansing, sanctification, divine healing and many more spiritual blessings in Christ. The atoning work on the cross offers us complete wholeness in every aspect of life, both spiritually and physically. Adam's first fall plunged mankind into a huge calamity – Christ's redemptive work places man in abundant life (John 10.10). Jesus is the light of the world (John 8.12) and His brightness gives us a bright and healthy life. "But unto you that fear my name shall the sun of righteousness arise with healing in his wings; and ye shall go forth, and grow up as calves of the stall" (Malachi 4.2). In Isaiah 53 the terms, 'griefs' and 'sorrows' point to physical afflictions. Both the spiritual aspect of the redemptive work on the cross which made provision for sin as well as the physical aspect, that made provision for sicknesses can be appropriated by faith. Even if an ailment is as a result of a curse, Jesus became a curse for us and took every curse upon Himself so that we may be liberated (Galatians 3.13). Jesus forgave sins and cast out devils, which were spiritual graces. Moreover, He healed sick and diseased bodies, which was the physical aspect. When Jesus came to the earth, He went about doing good by healing all kinds of illnesses and diseases even before He went to the cross, but eventually, the climax of it all was His atoning work at Calvary, which was a fulfillment of Isaiah 53. "That it might be fulfilled which was spoken by Esaias the prophet, saying, Himself took our infirmities, and bare our sicknesses" (Matthew 8.17). *"Whom God hath set forth to be a propitiation through faith in his blood" (Romans 3:25).*

A propitiation refers to the turning away of wrath through the offering of a sacrifice. When Christ died on the Cross He became a propitiation for our sins. "And He is the propitiation for our sins: and not for ours only, but also for the sins of the whole world" (1John 2:2). On the cross, He became a sacrifice for our sins. The penalty for Adam's sin and the sins of all mankind is death (Romans 6.23) but Jesus, who knew no sin, became sin for us (2nd Corinthians 5.21) and paid the penalty on the cross so we may have eternal life (John 3.16, Ephesians 2.1-5). Not only that, but through His death we can have many more spiritual blessings in Christ Jesus (Ephesians 1.3). The propitiation serves to reconcile us back to God and God to His people. The wrath of God was put on His only begotten Son instead of us. Judgment was supposed to be the portion of both the elect and the non-elect (Ephesians 2.3). God and man were on opposite ends and God was supposed to be angry with us and against us. A sacrificial lamb was required, such as the one introduced by John the Baptist as, "behold the Lamb of God, which taketh away the sin of the world" (John 1.29). Christ fit this position perfectly, as though He had been interviewed for a job and had fit the requirements perfectly; He was going to obey the Father and go to the cross to become a propitiation for the sins of Adam and his descendants. He bore the wrath of God that you and I were supposed to bear. Shouldn't this make us love Christ more and more due to His abundant grace?

All throughout the Old Testament we find that sacrifices were needed to atone for sins, including the sacrifice that was made all the way in Genesis 3 when God made coats of skins for Adam and Eve to cover them after they had fallen. This was achieved through the shedding of the blood of an innocent animal in order to make atonement for their sin and reconcile them to Himself, exonerating them from His wrath. When the Israelites had sinned against God and had constructed a Golden Calf in Moses' absence, God said to Moses, "now therefore let me alone, that my wrath may wax hot against them, and that I may consume them" (Exodus 32:10). Moses became a mediator between God and the people saying to God, "why doth thy wrath wax hot against thy people, which thou hast brought forth out of the land of Egypt with great power, and with a mighty hand?" (Exodus 32:11). The Bible tells us, "and the LORD repented of the evil which he thought to do unto his people" (Exodus 32:14). In a similar manner, Abraham negotiated and pleaded with God so that Sodom and Gomorrah may be spared (Genesis 18.22-33). Moreover, when Korah and his associates rebelled against God and He wanted to judge them with a plague, Moses said to

Aaron, "take a censer, and put fire therein from off the altar, and put on incense, and go quickly unto the congregation, and make an atonement for them: for there is wrath gone out from the LORD; the plague is begun. And Aaron took as Moses commanded, and ran into the midst of the congregation; and, behold, the plague was begun among the people: and he put on incense, and made an atonement for the people. And he stood between the dead and the living; and the plague was stayed." (Numbers 16:46-48).

The plague was stopped due to the intercession and the atonement made by Aaron. "For if, when we were enemies, we were reconciled to God by the death of his Son, much more, being reconciled, we shall be saved by his life" (Romans 5:10). Now that we have been reconciled, we can say, "and in that day thou shalt say, O LORD, I will praise thee: though thou wast angry with me, thine anger is turned away, and thou comfortedst me" (Isaiah 12:1). Because of the reconciliation wrought by God through His only begotten Son Jesus Christ, God's wrath has been diverted from us and we have been reconciled to Him (2nd Corinthians 5.18). Now we are candidates for salvation and healing; favour is now our portion because through Christ we, "have access by one Spirit unto the Father" (Ephesians 2:18). This should cause us to run to God because of the immense love He has shown us - "we love Him, because he first loved us" (1 John 4:19).

The law of Moses was not given to man to be a mechanism to save him from sin but rather to serve as a kind of mirror which would make him know his sin. When Adam had to leave the Garden of Eden, he was made to know that he could only approach a Holy God through the offering of sacrifices (Genesis 3.15, 4.4, 21). When the High Priest of Israel entered the Holy of Holies, yearly on the Day of Atonement, sin was transferred to an animal without blemish, which would give the person who sinned the status of right standing before God. The animal being slain was serving as a type of Christ who would serve as a substitute for the sinner that calls upon Him in faith, taking the role of a mediator between God and man. "Through His name, whoever believes in Him will receive remission of sins" (Acts 10:43).

When the apostles were facing much resistance as they preached about the work of Jesus on the cross and about His resurrection, they faced much persecution which made them pray for power that would enable them to continue preaching the gospel. "Now, Lord, look on their threats, and grant to your servants that with all boldness they may speak your word, by stretching out your hand to heal, and that signs and wonders may be done through the name of your Holy Servant Jesus" (Acts 4:29-30). Their prayers were answered when they were filled with the Holy Ghost and with boldness which, enabled them to preach the gospel more effectively, with signs and wonders following. They were able to preach the Gospel of Christ and perform similar works as Jesus did. "There came also a multitude out of the cities round about unto Jerusalem, bringing sick folks, and them which were vexed with unclean spirits: and they were healed every one" (Acts 5.16).

 The gospel spread and the Kingdom of God expanded through the preaching of the apostles and the signs and wonders that Christ did through them. When Paul was preaching at one time, He taught that Christ, the son of David, would show them mercy after being resurrected. Surely, God forgave and healed many people as can be seen in Paul's ministry at Lystra and Iconium, for example. Those mercies would include the forgiveness of sins and the healing of diseases. God forgave and healed then and He still forgives and heals now. Churches should teach on healing to increase the faith of the church so they can receive their healing. Faith comes by hearing (Romans 10.17), so the more divine healing is taught, the more the church members will be able to get the faith to receive their healing. Furthermore, in the history of the church, a number of healing revivals have taken place, which were successful in creating the awareness of divine healing, as well as getting many people healed and adding souls to the church. More revivals are needed in our day. The same Holy Spirit which, worked with Christ, the apostles and the members of the early church is still with us today; healing took place then and can still take place now. Jesus said of the Holy Ghost, "He shall glorify me: for he shall receive of mine, and shall shew it unto you" (John 16:14). The Holy Ghost was sent to the church in its fullness and power when the believers were gathered in the Upper Room (Acts 2.1-4). The Holy Ghost is still here to show us that healing and the works of Christ are still available in the church today. The Holy Ghost is a Helper and a Comforter (John 14.16), thus all who are sick can receive the comfort that He is here to help and heal them. Do not condemn yourself; the same faith you have in His atoning work on the cross can be translated into faith for your healing as well because on the cross he died for both your sins and your sicknesses.

One time when Bartimaeus, the blind man heard that Jesus would be passing by, he called onto Him saying, "Jesus, thou Son of David, have mercy on me" (Mark 10.47). After he told Jesus that he wanted healing so he could see again, Jesus told him that he had been healed due to his faith. After he had received his sight instantly, he saw Jesus and started following Him. Some say seeing is believing, but in God's scheme of things, 'believing is seeing.' Do you have the faith to go for your healing? God is your doctor and the medicine He prescribes is His Word [Psalms 107:20, John 1:14].

Christ – the Lamb that was slain

When we read the Bible, many pictures of Christ are painted in the Old Testament. In the Book of Exodus, we find a picture of the crucifixion of Christ painted as the

Passover. The night before the Israelites were to leave Egypt, an angel was sent to bring death to all their firstborns, both man and beast. However, the houses with the blood of the Passover lamb on their doorposts would be spared. There are some striking similarities between the Passover and the crucifixion of Christ on the Cross. The Passover sacrifice was to be selected on the 10th day of the tenth month of Nisan on the Hebrew calendar (Exodus 12.3). In a similar fashion, Jesus rode into Jerusalem for the Passover on the 10th day of the month of Nisan as a lamb selected for the sacrifice (John 1.29, John 12.12-14). Blood was to be placed on the lentils and the doorposts, forming horizontal and vertical lines that are typical of a cross (Exodus 12.21-23). Similarly, Jesus died on a cross and shed his blood for the redemption of mankind (Hebrews 9.12). The bones of the Passover lamb were not to be broken; not even one (Exodus 12.46). In a similar fashion, not even one of Jesus' bones was broken as He hang on the cross (John 19.32-36). The people of Israel were redeemed from bondage when they escaped from Egypt on the 15th of Nisan (Exodus 12.29-42). Jesus died on the cross on the 15th of Nisan, redeeming and saving humanity from sin (John 18.28). He was crucified on the exact day of the Passover. The Passover lamb was eaten at the Passover feast so that they may have life (Exodus 12.8,13). Similarly, in the New Covenant, we have life when we eat Jesus' flesh (John 6.50-58). The sacrifice of the Passover Lamb was representative of God's plan of salvation for the nation of Israel (Exodus 12.13). The sacrifice of Christ was God's plan of salvation for man (John 3.1-16). An interesting fact about the Passover and the Exodus is that you needed to eat it, "with your loins girded, your shoes on your feet, and your staff in your hand; and ye shall eat it in haste: it is the LORD'S Passover" (Exodus 12.11). This means that the lamb that was slain is readily available to rescue you and get you out of your negative situation in haste. The question is, 'are you ready?'

Healing is a part of the inheritance – Christ gives us forgiveness for the soul and healing for our bodies. He was wounded for our transgressions and bruised for our iniquities. Moreover, with his stripes we are healed. When unleavened cakes were being prepared, they were burnt and holes were made in them. In a similar fashion, Christ's back was lashed, His body was pierced and the judgement of God fell upon Him. Jesus was an unblemished lamb just as the lamb that was used for the Passover was unblemished. The Pharisees, the scribes, Caiaphas and Pilate examined Jesus in Jerusalem for four days before His execution. Afterwards, Pilate declared him clean on three separate occasions. He rode into Jerusalem five days before the lamb was slaughtered in the temple to serve as the Passover sacrifice for the sins of Israel. The lamb was chosen five days before it was sacrificed. This means, Jesus entered Jerusalem on the very day that the lamb was selected as the Lamb of God. The people waved their palm branches and shouted 'Hosanna' which means 'save us.'

Unfortunately, the people were looking for a political Savior and not a spiritual one, so Jesus wept as He entered the city.

Jesus was indeed crucified on the Passover. The priest in the temple would blow the shofar (or the Ram's horn) at 3 in the afternoon at the time the lamb was to be sacrificed. At this moment, the people of Israel would think about the substitutionary sacrifice for their sins. Jesus said, 'it is finished,' when He was crucified at exactly 3pm on the day of the Passover, at the time when the shofar was blown. Christ was crucified at the exact time that the Passover lamb would be slaughtered for the sins of the people - Christ is the Lamb of God that was slain. At that very moment, the veil that separated the Holy Place from the Holy of Holies was torn from top to bottom - the separation between God and man had been torn away. Now all can, "come boldly to the throne of grace, that we may obtain mercy and find grace to help in time of need" (Hebrews 4.16).
Paul clearly referred to Jesus as our Passover in 1st Corinthians 5.7, "for even Christ our Passover is sacrificed for us" (1st Corinthians 5.7). We need to place the blood of Christ on the doorposts of our heart for our protection.

Chapter 3: Change your mind about healing

"'But if you can do anything, have compassion on us and help us.' Jesus said to him, 'if you can believe, all things are possible to him who believes'" (Mark 9:22, 23)
The people hang upon the compassion that was in Jesus to draw healing from Him. He has compassion to heal you too. He healed then and still heals now. It is a sad thing to know that some people think that miracles are not for today. The Father loves us and wants us to be healed. The truth of healing is a special grace of the kingdom and Jesus is willing to give it. We have an even better Covenant now, so in fact, miracles and healing should even be more prevalent in our day than in olden times. But unfortunately, many people are perishing through a lack of knowledge about the wonderful benefits of the healing graces of Christ. Some have even not been taught about Christ as a healer. It should be noted that faith comes by hearing and thus many should be taught about the healing aspect of the Gospel. After hearing, perceive it with your eye of faith. Apart from being taught in our churches, parents should also teach their children about Jesus and His ability to heal the sick. Don't feel condemned if you are sick, there is

healing available in Christ. Most of the works of Christ were those of healing – Jesus healed wherever He went. "Which of you by worrying can add one cubit to his stature" (Mathew 6.27). Why worry when you can experience the Master's healing touch. In order to experience the wonderful benefits of the healing power that can be drawn from Christ and to have the faith that can appropriate it, it would be good to live our lives according to the Word of God and depend on the power of the Holy Spirit to walk victoriously. The 'rapha' which appears in Genesis 20.17 refers to the healing of a physical condition. Jehovah-Rapha is standing by to heal you.

Healing and the kingdom

"He saith unto them, they that are whole have no need of the physician, but they that are sick" (Mark 2:17). Many people are sick in the world and the church today because they don't know the Good News about healing. No wonder the Bible says, "my people are destroyed for lack of knowledge" (Hosea 4:6). Knowledge about the truth of divine healing is very necessary because "wisdom and knowledge shall be the stability of thy times" (Isaiah 33.1). There are two main aspects of this; firstly, in Matthew 10.7-8, Jesus exhorted His followers and still exhorts us to, "preach, saying, the kingdom of heaven is at hand. Heal the sick, cleanse the lepers, raise the dead, cast out devils: freely ye have received, freely give." It seems most of the people in the church have not brought themselves to accept the truth that healing is a part of the kingdom message as has been shown in this scripture. Secondly, this truth about divine healing might not be taught in many churches. A lack of teaching on the subject leads to an inability to come to terms with this Biblical truth because it is not taught. As a result, the people would not have the knowledge of it and would not be able to exercise the faith for divine healing because, "faith cometh by hearing, and hearing by the word of God" (Romans 10:17). Divine healing must be taught in our churches so that many would know that it is a grace that is available to them. Moreover, some teachers assert that divine healings were accomplished in the time of the early church and the apostles and have ceased today. But this is largely untrue as we have witnessed so many miraculous healings that have taken place in our times within the ministries of servants of God such as John G Lake, Smith Wigglesworth, William Branham, John Alexander Dowie, Kathryn Kuhlman, Oral Roberts, Dag Heward-Mills, Benny Hinn and many others.

Furthermore, many people in the church are behaving like Pharisees and are stopping people in the church from getting their healing because of how they view their Christian life. Just as some Pharisees were not in support of Jesus' healing and casting out devils at certain times, because it was not in accordance to the law, certain legalistic Christians make it difficult for other Christians to pursue their healing because they may see those Christians as 'unqualified' for their miracles. This is indeed awful because Christ forgave sins and healed diseases. If there is someone in the church you think is not 'qualified' for healing, please do not condemn such a person but allow him to seek Christ for His healing because Christ has the power to forgive sins and to heal all manner of diseases.

Kenneth Hagin spoke about how some church members would tell him God would not help someone because the person had sinned; Pastor Hagin prayed for the person and the person got healed. Sometimes they even had a problem with Pastor Hagin because he prayed for that Cristian. But he would think, 'I happen to know that he has sinned. But did they happen to know he had repented?' Kenneth Hagin said the mercy of God amazed him and that sometimes he prayed for some people in the church whom he thought would not get healed - but they were and that he prayed for other good church members and they didn't get healed. In another instance, he saw that the Spirit of God was using a man to do healings, but he knew some faults about the man. He asked God about this and God told him that he didn't believe in his own preaching. God then referred him to a time when he was preaching out of Isaiah 43 and said, 'I, am he that blotted out thy transgressions for mine own sake, and I will not remember thine iniquities.' God then told him that the fellow was someone He had touched because he had confessed and had asked for forgiveness. Kenneth Hagin then got the revelation that God does not remember confessed sin, but we humans do. "I, even I, am he that blotteth out thy transgressions for mine own sake, and will not remember thy sins. Put me in remembrance: let us plead together: declare thou, that thou mayest be justified" (Isaiah 43:25-26). God then spoke to Pastor Hagin about a female minister that he had asked about since that woman seemed to have a clean record. Pastor Hagin wanted to know why God hadn't used that woman instead. God told Him that things seemed to be clean with the woman on the outside but that woman had been disobedient to God for 40 years. God had spoken to her to do certain things and she didn't do them though she came to church and seemed to live an upright life. God then contrasted this woman with the man who had done wrong and had repented. Kenneth Hagin was then satisfied. Some people might have made some mistakes but if they have repented, God doesn't hold those mistakes against them any longer and doesn't see them. "And the prayer of faith shall save the sick, and the Lord shall raise him up; and if he have committed sins, they shall be forgiven him" (James 5:15).

By this, sin is not being encouraged but you need to know the truth which will make you free (John 8.32), because the devil doesn't want you to know the truth and that's because he is a liar (John 8.44). If you are sick and are being told that you wouldn't get healing from God because of something you have done and have repented of, don't be discouraged but continue to pursue

God and your healing with faith and God will touch you. Believe the Bible and believe in what God has said and do not doubt. The devil introduced doubt into the mind of Eve when she was in the Garden of Eden and thereby robbed her, as well as Adam, of their blessings. The Word of God is the Sword of the Spirit and it can cut through every deception of the devil.

When Kenneth Hagin believed he would receive his healing because He had seen it in the Word of God, he was accused of being a fanatic, but he continued to pursue it and finally received it from God. He received the revelation of healing from the Bible and run with and it and it surely worked for Him. "The entrance of thy words giveth light" (Psalm 119:130). He began teaching about healing in his church and people began to be healed too. Healing worked for him and it can work for you too. Kenneth Hagin again spoke about a crippled lady who needed healing. He opened his Bible while sitting by her to 1st Peter 2.24 which says, "who his own self bare our sins in his own body on the tree, that we, being dead to sins, should live unto righteousness: by whose stripes ye were healed." He then asked the woman, "is the Word 'were' past tense, future tense, or present tense?" The woman lit up and said, 'it's past tense. And if we WERE healed, I WAS!" Pastor Hagin then told her to lift up her hands and praised God because she had been healed. The woman smiled and lifted up her hands to praise God and began to tell him how happy she was to be healed as well as how she wasn't helpless and so forth. She said this while she was crippled and still couldn't walk. Pastor Hagin then told the whole congregation to lift up their hands and praise God with her because she had received healing and they did so, but the woman was still in a crippled state. When they stopped praising, Kenneth Hagin told her, "now, my sister, rise and walk in Jesus' name!" Immediately, the woman jumped up and danced around the room – she had been healed. She had been healed several years ago (1st Peter 2.24) but found out that night.

"When Jesus saw their faith, he said unto the sick of the palsy, son, thy sins be forgiven thee. But there were certain of the scribes sitting there, and reasoning in their hearts, why doth this man thus speak blasphemies? Who can forgive sins but God only? And immediately when Jesus perceived in his spirit that they so reasoned within themselves, he said unto them, why reason ye these things in your hearts? Whether is it easier to say to the sick of the palsy, thy sins be forgiven thee; or to say, arise, and take up thy bed, and walk? But that ye may know that the Son of man hath power on earth to forgive sins, (he saith to the sick of the palsy,) I say unto thee, arise, and take up thy bed, and go thy way into thine house (Mark 2:5-11).

Another group that brought resistance to divine healings were the Sadducees. The Sadducees were a Jewish sect that were in the higher echelons of society. One main thing that characterized this group is that they did not believe in the supernatural or in miracles. On one occasion when God healed a man through Peter and John, the Sadducees who did not believe in miracles were stunned and said, "what shall we do to these men? For that indeed a notable miracle hath been done by them is manifest to all them that dwell in Jerusalem; and we cannot deny it. But that it spread no further among the people, let us straitly threaten them, that they speak henceforth to no man in this name. And they called them, and commanded them not to speak at all nor teach in the name of Jesus" (Acts 4:16-18). The Sadducees were so much opposed to the supernatural acts of the Holy Spirit that they wanted to find a way to put a stop to the apostles. In order for supernatural Acts of the Holy Spirit such as healings and miracles to take place, we need not have the anti-miracle mindset of the Sadducees, but wholly embrace the reality of the Holy Spirit and His supernatural works.

The fact of the matter is that, God wants to heal YOU - that is one of the reasons Jesus came. He came to bring salvation, which includes your healing. Salvation is a complete package. Even before Jesus came to the earth, God was healing the divers diseases of the Israelites (Exodus 15.26). When Jesus came to the earth, He continued the work of healing through the power of the Holy Spirit. He said, "the Spirit of the Lord is upon me, because he hath anointed me to preach the gospel to the poor; he hath sent me to heal the brokenhearted, to preach deliverance to the captives, and recovering of sight to the blind, to set at liberty them that are bruised" (Luke 4.18). Healing was a part of the mandate of Jesus and the announcement of this mandate by Him was a confirmation of what Isaiah prophesied in Isaiah 61.1. He also cast out evil spirits through the agency of the Holy Spirit (Matthew 12.28). The climax of it all was when He went on the cross of the Calvary to bear our sins and sicknesses upon Himself (Isaiah 53.4-5). Afterwards, He sent the same Holy Spirit to empower the apostles and all believers to continue the work, relying on the power of the Holy Spirit. The same Holy Spirit is with us today to perform healings as in the time of the early church. The Holy Spirit has been sent by Jesus to be with us to comfort, help and heal us. If you are sick, be encouraged because Jesus has made the provision for you to attain your healing.

The same God who was and is the healer of Israel is the same God who is your healer. In Psalm 103, we find the following passage:

"Bless the LORD, O my soul: and all that is within me, bless his holy name. Bless the LORD, O my soul, and forget not all his benefits: who forgiveth all thine iniquities; who healeth all thy diseases; Who redeemeth thy life from destruction; who crowneth thee with lovingkindness and tender mercies; Who satisfieth thy mouth with good things; so that thy youth is renewed like the eagle's. The LORD executeth righteousness and judgment for all that are oppressed. He made known his ways unto Moses, his acts unto the children of Israel. The LORD is merciful and gracious, slow to anger, and plenteous in mercy. He will not always chide: neither will he keep his anger forever. He hath not dealt with us after our sins; nor rewarded us according to our iniquities. For as the heaven is high above the earth, so great is his mercy toward them that fear him. As far as the east is from the west, so far hath he removed our transgressions from us. Like as a father pitieth his children, so the LORD pitieth them that fear him. For he knoweth our frame; he remembereth that we are dust" (Psalm 103:1-14).

Do not forget His benefits. There are many benefits from serving the Lord and one of them is that of healing. He forgives all your iniquities and heals all your diseases. Yes, all your diseases! The scripture quoted above says it all. Though the Israelites had been disobedient, God was going to forgive their disobedience and would heal them. They would then know His immense love and grace and would willingly turn to Him. At certain times, the Israelites took themselves out of the protection of God's Covenant with them. God had wished that they had always remained in it so that they would be beneficiaries of His covenant continually, but sometimes the people missed the mark. Because of sin, the devil had every right to afflict them with disease, however, when they turned back to God, He forgave them and healed them. According to the healing covenant in Exodus 15.26, the Lord wishes all to be well but there are some conditions attached. Obedience to Him and His Word are required. It would be important to listen to His voice; to be obedient and walk in the fruit of the Spirit and to value the teachings in the Scriptures. Psalm 107 also tells us that, "because of their transgression, and because of their iniquities, are afflicted............Then they cry unto the LORD in their trouble, and he saveth them out of their distresses. He sent his word, and healed them, and delivered them from their destructions" (Psalm 107.17,19-20).

Jesus had not even come to die on the cross when Israel were beneficiaries of the healing blessings of God - they knew a Saviour was coming to them but He had not come yet. Now that He has come and has performed His redemptive work on the cross, the healing blessings are even in much more abundance. "I am come that they might have life, and that they might have it more abundantly" (John 10:10). The New Covenant God has established with Israel and the church (Jeremiah 31.31, Luke 22.20) has even better promises (Hebrews 8.6) including the Promise of healing. It's time to receive your healing by faith from God. In James 5.14, he asks, "is any sick among you?" This question may have been a question of surprise because James, the pastor of the church in Jerusalem might not have expected anyone to be sick. The same Jesus who healed then still heals now. God wishes that we never become sick and that we remain in health till we grow to a ripe old age. He says, "beloved, I wish above all things that thou mayest prosper and be in health, even as thy soul prospereth" (3 John 1:2). Jesus is abounding in mercy and don't allow the mistakes of your past to stop you from pursuing Him to receive the forgiveness and the healing you need. "If ye then, being evil, know how to give good gifts unto your children, how much more shall your Father which is in heaven give good things to them that ask him?" (Matthew 7:11). One of the names of God is Jehovah-Jireh, which means, "the Lord will provide" (Genesis 22.14). When God told Abraham to sacrifice Isaac on the mount and Abraham obeyed, God later showed grace and provided a ram, which would be used as the sacrifice instead of Isaac. Abraham then named the place of the sacrifice, 'Jehovah-Jireh,' because God had graciously provided a sacrifice to be used in place of Isaac. God is a Father who provides for His children and one of the things He provides is healing. Why does He want to provide healing? One of the reasons is that He knows that if you are unhealthy, you wouldn't be able to have a wholesome and fulfilling life. "Trust............in the living God, who giveth us richly all things to enjoy" (1 Timothy 6:17). Yes, the Gospel is the Good News of Jesus Christ and He wants to provide you with healing as part of that gospel.

Jesus is indeed willing to heal. The Scriptures teach us that He is willing to do so (Matthew 8.3) and our faith is required to receive the healing. In the case of the leper, he knew Jesus certainly had the ability to heal Him. He said, 'thou canst make me clean.' (Matthew 8:2). But was

Jesus willing? He indeed was - "I am willing; be cleansed" (Matthew 8:3). If He did it for this man, He would do it for you too. In God's name as 'Jehovah-Rapha', He reveals Himself as a healer, one of His many attributes. When Jesus said it is finished, it was a once-and-for-all victory for us all. Since healing is provided as part of God's Covenant, we can ask for it because He has made that provision a part of the Covenant. In Exodus 15.26, God showed that healing was part of His Covenant with them. When we want to petition God for something, we can look through the Scriptures to see if the things we are asking for can be found in it. Moreover, we must also check and see if we are fulfilling the conditions that would deliver the promise. Christ has done His part through His atoning work on the cross, but do we walk in faith and obedience so we can appropriate those promises? If we are unsure about what God has promised us and what we can do to appropriate those blessings, we can pray for more revelation on the matter. God's general will is stated in the scriptures and a deeper study of the Word will reveal the general will of God to us.

Being well acquainted with the Bible will familiarize us with the general will of God as expounded therein. Apart from the general will, there is also God's specific will, which has to do with the choices we make in our day-to-day life. In order to know God's specific will on certain matters, prayer can help in this regard, "making request if, by some means, now at last I may find a way in the will of God to come to you" (Romans 1:10). Prayer in the spirit can be especially beneficial to living a Spirit-led life as one becomes conscious of the indwelling of the Holy Spirit (Ezekiel 36.27). "But the anointing which you have received from Him abides in you, and you do not need that anyone teach you; but as the same anointing teaches you concerning all things" (1st John 2:27).

Exodus 15.26 spells out God's healing Covenant with Israel. When the Israelites were fleeing from Egypt and had crossed the Red Sea, they arrived in the wilderness and then travelled for three days without water. They then arrived at an oasis called Marah, but the water there was so bitter that they could not drink of it. Consequently, the people complained and Moses prayed to God about the situation. God then showed them a tree whose branches would be used for healing when it was cast into the bitter water. This would sweeten the water and would heal it of its bitterness. Like that bitter oasis, many situations and experiences in life can be very bitter for us. Some of those bitter experiences include sickness. When we cast our burden of sickness upon him, he can provide the healing that would turn the bitter situation to sweetness. Furthermore, God led the people to a place called Eli where they found twelve wells of water and seventy palm trees. Twelve is the number of government and seventy represents the impartation of God's Spirit, increase and restoration

(Numbers 11.13-17). The bitter waters of Marah had turned into sweetness and also increase and restoration.

The mind is a battlefield and you need to know and understand that healing is for you because it is a part of God's programme of redemption and salvation. The devil wants to rob you of your healing because he is a liar (John 8.44) and works through deception (Revelation 12.9). He is an accuser (Rev 12.10) and wants to leave you in a sickly state so that he can accuse you of being a sick and an unworthy Christian. Do not be consumed by fear of being left sick because of your previous lifestyle before you repented. Job said, "for the thing which I greatly feared is come upon me, and that which I was afraid of is come unto me" (Job 3:25). Renew your mind to accept the truths of this New and better Covenant (Hebrews 8.6). Paul frequently emphasized the renewal of mind of born-again Christians (Ephesians 4.23, Romans 12.2). Change your mind from how Adam thinks to how Christ thinks now that you are born-again. Christ thinks healing is possible. Remove erroneous and legalistic teachings from your minds and realize that though you may have had some struggles and may have made some mistakes in the past, if you repent and seek God and His healing touch, you will be healed. God has invited us to His table of forgiveness and healing. He says, "come now, and let us reason together, ...though your sins be as scarlet, they shall be as white as snow; though they be red like crimson, they shall be as wool. If ye be willing and obedient, ye shall eat the good of the land" (Isaiah 1:18-19). Even sins that are as red as scarlet can be forgiven by God if we repent and walk in obedience because God is, "the LORD God, merciful and gracious, longsuffering, and abundant in goodness and truth, keeping mercy for thousands, forgiving iniquity and transgression and sin" (Exodus 34:6-7). Are you looking to him for forgiveness and healing, "every good gift and every perfect gift is from above" (James 1:17). You can ask him for healing by faith and He will do it for you (John 14.14).

The Woman with the issue of Blood

Many people might be familiar with the account of the woman with the issue of blood in the Bible. The Holy Spirit has many truths to reveal to us in this account. First, Jesus performed this miracle while He was on His way to raise Jairus' daughter from the dead. Jesus is full of grace and has time for all His loved ones. He doesn't mind attending to you if you need healing, even if it seems to you that He is attending to other issues. It should also to be noted that the woman had suffered with this issue of blood for a long time. "And a woman having an issue of blood twelve years, which had spent all her living upon physicians, neither could be healed of any" (Luke 8:43). Not only had she suffered for 12 years, but she had also spent much money going to physicians who could not help her. This is the case with some of you. You may have had certain diseases for a long time and the physicians might not know what is going on with you; this could be an indication that your ailment could be as a result of a spirit of infirmity. The good news is that Jesus has the cure. The woman had probably heard that Jesus was going about doing good and healing all manner of sicknesses through the agency of the Holy Spirit (Acts 10.38). Since she had heard of the works of Jesus, she exercised the faith to go to Him for healing, because faith comes by hearing (Romans 10.17). Her faith was so strong that she believed that even if she touched the hem of Jesus' garment, she would be healed. As soon as she touched Him, the issue of blood was healed instantly (Luke 8.44).

The hem is known in Jewish culture to be the place where authority is signified. It also showed that the Jews had a special relationship with God (Numbers 15.37-40, Deuteronomy 22.12). In touching the hem of the garment, the woman was showing two things; that she believed in the authority of Jesus and His ability to heal her and that Christ had a special relationship with God – in this case, Christ was the Son of God. The faith of the woman was further demonstrated when she found her way to Jesus to touch Him in spite of the many people who had gathered around Him who were also in search of healing or some other kind of miracle from Him (Luke 8.45). Many come to the church of God and get involved in religious activities and ceremonies but don't actually, touch Him. This touch was a special touch of faith which made Jesus respond by saying, 'who touched me' (Luke 8:45). The woman tried to hide, wanting the healing to be a secret, but Jesus knew that virtue had left him. Jesus knows all who need healing – nothing is hidden from Him (Isaiah 29.15). "Nathanael said to Him, 'how do you know me?' Jesus answered and said to him, 'before Philip called you, when you were under the fig tree, I saw you'" (John 1.48). As soon as Adam tried to hide from Him, God called unto Him and said, "where art thou?" (Genesis 3.9). Also, Elisha said to Gehazi, "'where did you go, Gehazi?' And he said, 'your servant did not go anywhere.' Then he said to him, 'did not my heart go with you'" (2nd Kings 5:25-26). He knows everything about you, "Jesus.........knew all men, and needed not that any should testify of man: for he knew what was in man" (John 2:24-25).

The woman came out of hiding, afraid that Jesus would be angry with her, not knowing the extent of the immense amount of grace and mercy He had in Him. Under normal circumstances, she was not even supposed to approach Him because she was ceremonially unclean due to the issue of blood - "if a woman has a discharge, and the discharge from her body is blood, she shall be set apart seven days; and whoever touches her shall be unclean until evening" (Leviticus 15:19). The woman can be compared to an 'unclean' sinner who reaches out to Christ to receive pardon, as well as healing. The Physicians did not have the power to forgive sins and heal the sin condition of man. Life is in blood (Leviticus 17.11) and the fact that she was losing it meant she was dying spiritually and physically. She had wanted to remain hidden, but the Saviour revealed her and spared her; she confessed and He comforted her and blessed her - "daughter, be of good cheer; your faith has made you well. Go in peace" (Luke 8:48).

The Healing of the two blind men

Jesus was going about doing good when 2 blind men saw him and called unto him for healing. They cried to him asking for mercy. The first question Jesus asked them was, "do you believe that I am able to do this?"(Matthew 9:28). He was testing their faith. When they said yes, He touched their eyes and said to them, "according to your faith let it be to you" (Matthew 9:29). Consequently, their eyes opened. Sin is a form of blindness (Deuteronomy 28.29, Isaiah 59.10, Zephaniah 1.17). Deliverance from sin is a removal of the blindness of sin (Isaiah 29.18, Isaiah 42.18, Isaiah 43.8, Ephesians 5.8). Jesus is the light of the world (John 8.12, John 9.5) and the light in Him delivers us from sin. "To open their eyes, in order to turn them from darkness to light, and from the power of Satan to God, that they may receive forgiveness of sins and an inheritance among those who are sanctified by faith in me" (Acts 26:18). He also heals our diseases because He is Jehovah-Rapha. Therefore, we can have both forgiveness of sin and healing of diseases. It is also interesting to note that though the two blind men could not see - they were able to know that He was the Promised Messiah though the Jews didn't. They saw Him with the eye of faith and that helped them to receive their healing. Jesus told them not to tell anyone of this miracle out of humility but perhaps, it was good that they did.

The healing of the paralytic

Jesus was teaching on a certain day and it so happened that there were some Pharisees sitting around there (Luke 5.17). Avenues to the healing of this paralytic were being blocked because the legalists were close-by - "they could not find how they might bring him in, because of the crowd" (Luke 5:19). Another avenue was sought. The men who were carrying the paralytic, "went up on the housetop and let him down with his bed through the tiling into the midst before Jesus" (Luke 5:19). They had to climb to the housetop to get past the blockade; faith climbs where we naturally cannot go (Matthew 17.20, Mark 9.23) and "let him who is on the housetop not go down" (Matthew 24:17). Their faith overcame the obstacles. David had the faith that the same God who had helped him to deal with the lion and the bear would deliver him out of the hands of Goliath (1st Samuel 17.36). As a result, he brought Goliath down with only a stone in a sling (1 Samuel 17.49) and "there was no sword in the hand of David" (1 Samuel 17.50). Jesus forgave them when He saw their faith even before they asked for healing. Now, "when He saw their faith, He said to him, man, your sins are forgiven you'" (Luke 5.20). The man was forgiven though there didn't seem to be any visible proof. God gives before we ask and better than we ask. Humanity has been plagued by sin and sickness results from it. The man's sin being forgiven carried even more weight than his sick condition; he needed peace in his conscience and now his conscience could finally be at rest. When the Pharisees opposed Jesus' willingness to forgive the man, He asked, "whether is easier, to say, thy sins be forgiven thee; or to say, rise up and walk?" (Luke 5:23).

 Jesus was going to the cross soon to perform His atoning work in order to deal with the sins of humankind because sin must be atoned for before He can fellowship with him. He was going to sweat blood in the Garden of Gethsemane before going to the cross. He had to endure harsh beatings and whips as he went to the cross and had to shed much blood on it to deal with the sins of mankind - "thy sins be forgiven thee" was harder to say than "rise up and walk?" The bodily healing would have helped him for his earthly life - the healing of his spirit through the atoning work of the cross would last into eternity (Ephesians 2.1). The problem of sin had to be dealt with on Calvary and when sin is dealt with, healing can come. At other times Jesus healed before He forgave, for example in the case of the man who had an infirmity for 38 years (John

5.14). Some people who were healed by Christ also became more receptive to the Gospel after they had been healed and this made it easier for them to receive forgiveness. Only Jesus has the power to forgive sins (Matthew 9.6, Mark 2.10, Luke 5.24). This paralytic had been in this condition for a long time and had probably gotten used to it. Sometimes this happens to people who are sick. The problem is that it creates a barrier to getting their healing because they become used to their predicament. But the kind of neighbours the paralytic had stirred him up again so he could go for his healing. The man must have also felt neglected since his condition might have kept him aloof. Furthermore, the religious enemies of Jesus, the Pharisees, had also created a religious blockade to the man's healing. When the man was seeking healing initially, his path had been blocked with many obstacles, but now, after his healing, the crowds gave him space to leave freely and all the people around were amazed" (Luke 5.26).

The healing of the Syrophenician woman

There was a certain woman who had a daughter that had an unclean spirit. The woman was a Caananite and more specifically, of Syrophenician (half Syrian, half Phoenician) origin. When she came to Jesus and asked Him to cast the devil out of her, Jesus "answered her not a word" (Matthew 15:23). Moreover, His disciples bid

Him to send her away. Jesus then replied, "I am not sent but unto the lost sheep of the house of Israel" (Matthew 15:24). The woman continued to pursue Jesus, but He replied, "it is not meet to take the children's bread and to cast it to dogs" (Matthew 15:26). The woman then replied, "truth, Lord: yet the dogs eat of the crumbs which fall from their masters' table" (Matthew 15.27).

First and foremost, this woman was a heathen Gentile and furthermore, a Canaanite. The Canaanites were a group of people that were heavily steeped in idolatry and were much opposed to the Israelites. When God wanted the Israelites to cross the Jordan and possess the Promised Land, that land was partly inhabited by Canaanites, which the Israelites had to defeat (Deuteronomy 7.2, Deuteronomy 20.17) in order to possess their land (Genesis 17.8). Caanan was also a son of Noah but unfortunately, he received a curse upon himself (Genesis 9.25) which also spread to his descendants, the Caananites, making them a cursed people. No wonder the disciples told Jesus to send this woman from Canaan away. In addition, Jesus commented that He was only sent to the house of Israel and that the children's bread should not be given to dogs. The term, 'dog' used here was meant to be contemptible (Deuteronomy 23.18, Job 30.1). The woman, unoffended by that term, however, still pursued the healing of her daughter and commented that the crumbs that fall from the master's table are eaten by the dogs. This is similar to what happened when the prodigal son had accepted his fault of leaving his father with his goods, which he later spent ill-advisedly and then came back to himself. "And when he came to himself, he said, how many hired servants of my father's have bread enough and to spare, and I perish with hunger! I will arise and go to my father, and will say unto him, Father, I have sinned against heaven, and before thee, and am no more worthy to be called thy son: make me as one of thy hired servants" (Luke 15:17-19). Like the Canaanite woman, he realized that his father had enough bread in his house but now that he had sinned, he felt unworthy to be treated well by his father and thought he should be treated as a hired servant who would eat crumbs from his father's table. She had heard of Jesus because He had been going around doing good. The Bible tells us, "and the fame of Him went out into every place of the country round about" (Luke 4:37).

She had asked him for mercy. The word, 'mercy' which is 'eleos, in the Greek, according to Strong's Concordance is defined as 'pity, mercy or compassion.' It also means 'kindness or good will towards the miserable and the afflicted with a desire to help them.' It is being exonerated from judgement that is deserved. "But go ye and learn what that meaneth, I will have mercy, and not sacrifice: for I am not come to call the righteous, but sinners to repentance" (Matthew 9:13). In another instance, Jesus also shows us how much He values mercy when He said, "but if ye had known what this meaneth, I will have mercy, and not sacrifice, ye would not have condemned the guiltless" (Matthew 12:7). Other scriptures such as Hosea 6.6, Matthew 23.23 also throw more light on God's mercy. Jesus had told her that the children need to be filled first and by the term, 'children' He was referring to the Jews. It seemed the woman didn't qualify, but little did she know, "that the Gentiles might glorify God for his mercy" (Romans 15:9). Her disqualification became her qualification due to His immense mercy. She continued to press on and she finally received the healing for her daughter, "Jesus answered and said to her, 'o woman, great is your faith! Let it be to you as you desire.' And her daughter was healed from that very hour" (Matthew 15.28). There is much to be learnt from this woman with regard to faith. The woman's steadfast faith had caused her to press on to receive her healing in spite of the seeming hurdles. Jesus has spread a table for us all - and all are invited. It doesn't matter what you have done in the past. You may feel unqualified but He invites you to, "come boldly unto the throne of grace, that we may obtain mercy, and find grace to help in time of need"(Hebrews 4.16).

Healing of Simon's Mother-in-law

Jesus came to Peter's house one time and saw that his mother-in-law lay there, sick. Jesus touched her and she received her healing. The touch was one of grace and compassion that energized her back to optimum health. It was an immediate healing as well. Though her sickness had been a big burden to her, the compassionate touch of Jesus brought her much rest. "Come unto me, all ye that labour and are heavy laden, and I will give you rest" (Matthew 11:28). It provided Him much joy to release people from the burden of sin and sickness due to His immense mercy. "But God, who is rich in mercy, for His great love wherewith he loved us" (Ephesians 2:4). "With everlasting kindness will I have mercy on thee" (Isaiah 54:8). He laboured throughout the day, doing good to all men (John 9.4) to the point that he sometimes became exhausted (John 4.6). But exhaustion did not deter Him in any way from doing the good works that God the Father had sent Him to the earth to perform (John 6.38). It was indeed a labour of love and in the same way, "God is not unrighteous to forget your work and labour of love, which ye have shewed toward his name, in that ye have ministered to the saints, and do minister" (Hebrews 6:10).

The healing of the man born blind

Jesus was passing by when He saw a man who had been blind from birth. Many knew him as a beggar on the streets of Jerusalem. The disciples too had heard about this man and asked Jesus, "master, who did sin, this man, or his parents, that he was born blind?" (John 9:2). This question shows what was on the mind of the disciples; they were linking the man's condition with the problem of sin. They were in a state of deliberation; could this have been the man's own doing (Ezekiel 18.20) or as a result of sins emanating from his ancestral line (Lamentations 5.7). The man could not have put himself in such a condition since he was born with it; his condition was also not as a result of the sins of his ancestors. "What mean ye, that ye use this proverb concerning the land of Israel, saying, the fathers have eaten sour grapes, and the children's teeth are set on edge?......The soul that sinneth, it shall die. The son shall not bear the iniquity of the father, neither shall the father bear the iniquity of the son" (Ezekiel 18:20). They certainly knew that there was a relationship between sin and sickness but this case was a little baffling because the man had been born with this predicament from the onset. Jesus answered them by saying, "neither hath this man sinned, nor his parents: but that the works of God should be made manifest in him" (John 9:3). The teleology and the end of the matter was that the plight, as well as the healing of this man was to show God's glory. Such as in Job's case when he was afflicted but eventually received, "twice as much as he had before" (Job 42:10), all going to God's glory. Moreover, this healing occurred on the Sabbath, the day that became a point of controversy raised by the Pharisees. According to the law, this healing shouldn't have taken place; according to grace it needed to be.

"I am come into this world, that they which see not might see" (John 9:39)

At a point in time, the apostles questioned Jesus because they wanted to know whether the condition of the man born blind was as a result of his own sins or his parents' sins. This situation was not dissimilar from the situation where Job was confronted by his three friends. Eliphaz the eloquent concluded that Job was suffering because he had sinned. Bildad the brutal held the view that Job was a hypocrite. Zophar the zealous declared that Job was wicked. The Lord, however, stated that they had, "darkened counsel with words without knowledge" (Job 38.2). It is the Lord Himself who knows why we go through the things that we go through and experience some of the ailments we suffer. The fourth character, Elihu, played the role of an intercessor and not a judge. Can you intercede for your friends that are sick? Furthermore, Job himself received a more speedy recovery when he prayed for his friends. "The Lord turned again the captivity of Job, when he prayed for his friends" (Job 42.10).

The Healing of the man with the withered hand

Jesus entered the Synagogue on a Sabbath day and noticed a man with a withered hand.

"And they watched him, whether He would heal him on the Sabbath day; that they might accuse him" (Mark 3:2). The Pharisees thought they were doing the right thing by being legalistic and finding fault so they could accuse Jesus, but unbeknown to them, they were being used by the devil in this manner (Proverbs 14.20). Jesus posed a question which struck their conscience, leaving them dumbfounded. He asked, "is it lawful to do good on the Sabbath days, or to do evil? To save life, or to kill? But they held their peace. And when he had looked round about on them with anger, being grieved for the hardness of their hearts, he saith unto the man, stretch forth thine hand. And he stretched it out: and his hand was restored whole as the other" (Mark 3:5). Jesus was showing them that it was the heart that was the key issue (Proverbs 4.23).

"Though I speak with the tongues of men and of angels, but have not love, I have become sounding brass or a clanging cymbal. And though I have the gift of prophecy, and understand all mysteries and all knowledge, and though I have all faith, so that I could remove mountains, but have not love, I am nothing. And though I bestow all

my goods to feed the poor, and though I give my body to be burned, but have not love, it profits me nothing. Love suffers long and is kind; love does not envy; love does not parade itself, is not puffed up; does not behave rudely, does not seek its own, is not provoked, thinks no evil; does not rejoice in iniquity, but rejoices in the truth; bears all things, believes all things, hopes all things, endures all things. Love never fails. But whether there are prophecies, they will fail; whether there are tongues, they will cease; whether there is knowledge, it will vanish away" (1st Corinthians 13.1-8).

The Pharisees had indeed laid aside the weightier matters such as mercy (Mathew 23.23). They should have taken into consideration Mark 12.30-31 which speaks about loving God and loving your neighbor. This healing was accomplished on the Sabbath showing that indeed, "the Sabbath was made for man, and not man for the Sabbath" (Mark 2:27).

Jesus is not partial. He loves all of His creation wanting all to be saved (2nd Peter 3.9) and all to be well (3 John 1.2). "And him that cometh to me I will in no wise cast out" (John 6:37). He is also willing to heal you (Luke 5.13). It is up to you to touch Him with your faith and life and health will flow from Him to you. Jesus ministers with compassion out of His heart and also with power (Acts 8.10). He did healings on the Sabbath day, which was a day of rest - a day on which no work was to be done according to Jewish law. Jesus' idea of rest was different, He worked on the Sabbath day to bring rest to the souls of men (Matthew 11.28). His labour on the Sabbath was a labour of love (Hebrews 6.10, 1 Thessalonians 1.3).

The man's hand was withered, atrophied and rendered lifeless in every sense of the word. It had lost its ability to move, attached to his body but hanging there, lifeless; motionless –impossible to be cured by the expertise of any physician. When the man stretched forth his hand at the bidding of our Lord, the hand was restored to its fullest ability. This hand that was dead was now alive; now he could render service with it, as it had been compassionately healed by Jesus.

The woman with the Spirit of infirmity

This healing was also done on a Sabbath day while Jesus was teaching in a Synagogue. "And, behold, there was a woman which had a spirit of infirmity eighteen years, and was bowed together, and could in no wise lift up herself" (Luke 13:11). The woman's predicament was not from natural sources, but was spiritual. Jesus told the Pharisees that it was needful that He heal this woman on the Sabbath day because she was one, "whom satan hath bound" (Luke 13:16). Her muscles had been placed in an uncomfortable contracted state, but since she was able to come to the Synagogue to worship, it must not have been as serious as some of the other cases recorded in the Gospels. Jesus spoke His words of healing and loosed her from her infirmity (Luke 13.12). "And He laid His hands on her: and immediately she was made straight, and glorified God" (Luke 13:13). The hands laid on her transmitted life from the Holy Spirit into this ailing body.

The Pharisees had wanted to put a stop to this work of grace and didn't want her to be loosed from her infirmity on the Sabbath. But Jesus confronted them, saying, "doth not each one of you on the sabbath loose his ox or his ass from the stall, and lead him away to watering?" (Luke13:15). They had no problem loosing their oxen and asses from the stalls, but didn't want this woman to be loosed from the burden of sin and the predicament of her infirmity. God would have taken care of their oxen (Luke 12.6). They were also usually tied up for only a few hours; this woman had been tied up by the devil for 18 years. They would lead these animals to be watered but had a problem with sending this soul, which had been bound by satan to the well of living water (John 4.14). Jesus has given an open invitation to all men, telling them, "if any man thirst, let him come unto me, and drink" (John 7:37). They valued their oxen and asses more than a human soul in turmoil. The hearts of the Pharisees were hardened (Mark 10.5). However, God's intention for all mankind if they would allow Him is to "put a new spirit within...... and......take the stony heart out of their flesh, and......give them an heart of flesh" (Ezekiel 11:19).

When Jesus had made the Pharisees know that it was needful for this healing to take place on the Sabbath day and "when he had said these things, all his adversaries were ashamed: and all the people rejoiced for all the glorious things that were done by him" (Luke 13.17).

The healing of the man with dropsy

Jesus had gone to one of the houses of the Pharisees to eat. He knew how hardened in heart they were but Jesus likes to win all manner of souls and thus He accepted an invitation to eat in the house of a Pharisee. It was not a genuine invitation though; they were looking for an opportunity to find fault with him and accuse Him. "And, behold, there was a certain man before him which had the dropsy" (Luke 14:2). Dropsy, which is also called 'edema', is the swelling of soft tissues due to the accumulation of excess water. Jesus asked the Pharisees a very important question. "Is it lawful to heal on the Sabbath day?" (Luke 14:3). The Pharisees did not answer. Jesus took the man with dropsy, healed him and let him go. Jesus then asked the Pharisees another question, "which of you shall have an ass or an ox fallen into a pit, and will not straightway pull him out on the sabbath day?" (Luke 14:5). It can be inferred that the Pharisees valued oxen more than human souls because they attended to their oxen on the Sabbath but had a problem with human souls being attended to on that day. This is a very good point to chew upon; do we value human souls as much as we value other things. Do we love our neighbours as we love ourselves?

Healing of the 10 lepers

Jesus was going through a certain village when He sighted 10 lepers who stood afar off. From a long distance, they shouted, "Jesus, Master, have mercy on us" (Luke 17:13). These 10 banded together because they were in the same predicament (2 Kings 7.8). As we have seen, leprosy represented the sting of sin, which causes separation from God and thus, "stood afar off" (Luke 17:12). They were being obedient to the law, which restricted lepers from mingling with the common people (Leviticus 13.46, Numbers 5.2). Nonetheless, they had heard of Jesus and knew the abundant grace He carried within Him. As a result, they still called out to Him for mercy. With faith, they were able to lift up their voices, which probably, they might not have found easy to do because of their leprous condition. Faith would, however, rise above their present condition and circumstances so they would be able to get their healing. Jesus' treatment of this case was unique. Since the people stood afar off, it pointed to a weaker faith as compared to the woman who came close to touch the hem of His garment. Jesus asked the lepers to, "go shew yourselves unto the priests" (Luke 17:14). This was a test of their faith. Their faith served them well and was higher at this point because, "as they went, they were cleansed" (Luke 17:14). They were excited and well on their way off, but out of the 10, only 9 came back to thank Him, much grateful as a result of being released from the bondage and torment of sin and the predicament of sickness. The others had probably forgotten the weight of the law they had borne (Hebrews 12.1) and the yoke of the law they had been under (Matthew 11.29). Glory had not been given to God for His great mercy and love. The person who did come to Jesus to give thanks was a Samaritan, a Gentile who would have been thought least likely to render such an appreciation. When he came and gave thanks, Jesus told him, "arise, go thy way: thy faith hath made thee whole" (Luke 17:19). The word, 'whole' in the Greek is, 'sozo' which means, 'to save, to keep safe and sound, to recue from danger or destruction.' Not only had this man received healing, but now he received salvation for His soul as well due to his thanksgiving. This was an added benefit; the first was bodily healing – and now spiritual life.

"But we are bound to give thanks always to God for you, brethren beloved of the Lord, because God hath from the beginning chosen you to salvation through sanctification of the Spirit and belief of the truth" (2 Thessalonians 2:13). 10 is the number of law; leprosy is a representation of sin; "the strength of sin is the law" (1 Corinthians 15:56). These 10 lepers were healed by Jesus because, "the law was given by Moses, but grace and truth came by Jesus Christ" (John 1:17). Secondly, The Bible tells us, "and for the law of the Spirit of life in

Christ Jesus hath made me free from the law of sin and death" (Romans 8:2). Finally, it should be noted that, "a man is not justified by the works of the law, but by the faith of Jesus Christ, even we have believed in Jesus Christ, that we might be justified by the faith of Christ, and not by the works of the law: for by the works of the law shall no flesh be justified" (Galatians 2:16).

Book of Acts

God has given some members of the church the grace to heal others. In fact, all those who believe have the ability to heal. "And He said to them, 'and these signs will follow those who believe.........Go into all the world and preach the gospel to every creature.........lay hands on the sick, and they will recover'...... And they went out and preached everywhere, the Lord working with them and confirming the word through the accompanying signs" (Mark 16:15- 20). In the Book of Acts, we see many healings taking place through the apostles, as well as other members of the church. Mention is made of two deacons in the book that made very significant marks in the early church; one was named Philip and the other, Stephen. Many paralyzed people were healed through Philip's ministry, which was based primarily in Samaria. His healings of paralyzed people attracted many crowds and brought many people to Christ. Healing miracles created open doors and avenues for the Gospel to be spread. Many souls were won among the Jews as well as the Gentiles. The miracles of the apostles also won many to Christ. "And Peter said to him, 'Aeneas, Jesus the Christ heals you. Arise and make your bed.' Then he arose immediately. So all who dwelt at Lydda and Sharon saw him and turned to the Lord" (Acts 9:34-35).

Again at Lystra, there was a crippled man who needed healing. When Paul went there God made him know that the crippled man had the faith for healing. Paul commanded the man to stand up on His feet – an instruction to which the crippled man responded immediately, making him jump to his feet. The people around were astounded. Moreover, this healing miracle opened the door to the preaching of the Gospel in Lystra. As you can see, healing miracles open doors for the preaching of the Gospel. Furthermore, God used Paul to perform a lot of healings in Ephesus. "Now God worked unusual miracles by the hands of Paul, so that even handkerchiefs or aprons were brought from his body to the sick and the diseases left them and the evil spirits went out of them" (Acts 19:11-12). His ministry in Ephesus was the most impactful and made the Gospel spread to what was then known as Asia. Much evangelism took place in Malta due to the healing ministry of the Holy Spirit. As a result, many homes in Ephesus were used as meeting places of worship. This was a confirmation of the what the Lord had said, "but you shall receive power when the Holy Spirit has come upon you; and you shall be witnesses to Me in Jerusalem, and in all Judea and Samaria, and to the end of the earth" (Acts 1:8).

Paul's healing ministry in Malta was also very successful. "And it happened that the father of Publius lay sick of a fever and dysentery. Paul went in to him and prayed, and he laid his hands on him and healed him. So when this was done, the rest of those on the island who had diseases also came and were healed" (Acts 28:8-9). Though he had ended up on the island of Malta through a shipwreck, God turned the situation around for His divine purposes. All these healing miracles were accomplished through a heart of compassion.

Office gifts or Ministers are to act as equippers in order to equip the body of Christ to fulfill their God-given roles according to Ephesians 4.7-16. This would enable the saints to know who they are in Christ and what they have been called to do. Moreover, they need to be taught about the Holy Spirit and how He can work through them to use His gifts (gifts of the Spirit) to edify the church. The Christian minister needs to know that all healings need to be done in the name of Jesus.

The Healing of the Centurion's servant

A centurion had a servant who was sick and sent, "unto him the elders of the Jews, beseeching him that he would come and heal his servant" (Luke 7:3). He sent

Jews because he knew that there was a dividing line between Jew and Gentile and saw himself as unworthy to approach Jesus himself. The centurion had not gone after the pagan gods of Rome but had sought the one and only true God of Heaven. He also showed compassion for his servant and wanted to seek help for him. The people briefed Jesus about the situation, about how the centurion loved his nation and about how he had built a synagogue for worship, revealing his generosity. He agreed to go to the house with them. When Jesus had gotten close to his house, the centurion again, "sent friends to him, saying unto him, Lord, trouble not thyself: for I am not worthy that thou shouldest enter under my roof: Wherefore neither thought I myself worthy to come unto thee: But say in a word, and my servant shall be healed. For I also am a man set under authority, having under me soldiers, and I say unto one, Go, and he goeth; and to another, come, and he cometh; and to my servant, Do this, and he doeth it" (Luke 7:6-8). The centurion saw himself to be very unworthy as compared to the Holiness that characterized Christ. St Augustine commented on this by saying, 'counting himself unworthy that Christ should enter into his doors, he was counted worthy that Christ should enter into his heart.' This was a much better deal. The centurion showed forth a good heart and also much humility. He had also shown how much he understood authority. Since he was under authority himself, he knew how to respect authority and how to humble himself under it. He also knew that Christ's words had much authority that he didn't need Him to come to his house to accomplish the healing. "What manner of man is this! For He commandeth even the winds and water, and they obey him" (Luke 8.25). He just needed to speak a word for the healing to ensue. Not only that, he let Jesus know that he had people under his authority and was able to command them to do things for Him. If even he as a normal human being could utter words that carried enough authority to cause his subordinates to do this or that, how much more the words of God in the flesh; the king of kings. The man's humility and faith formed a double-edged sword. "When Jesus heard these things, he marvelled at him, and turned him about, and said unto the people that followed him, I say unto you, I have not found so great faith, no, not in Israel" (Luke 7:9). When the Centurion's entourage returned to the house, they found that the sick servant had been healed. Healed by what? By the authoritative Words of Jesus. "He sent his word, and healed them" (Psalm 107:20).

The Healing of the Nobleman's son

Jesus went to Cana, the place where he had turned water into wine. "And there was a certain nobleman, whose son was sick in Capernaum" (John 4:46). The man was a wealthy and notable man in society and hence, referred to in the Scriptures as a nobleman.

"When he heard that Jesus was come out of Judaea into Galilee, he went unto him, and besought him that he would come down, and heal his son: for he was at the point of death" (John 4:47). The nobleman seemed to be lacking in much faith when he wanted Jesus to come to his house and heal his son, which was a sharp contrast to the faith of the centurion who told Jesus, "I am not worthy that thou shouldest come under my roof: but speak the word only, and my servant shall be healed" (Matthew 8:8). Or in the case of Samuel who said, "speak; for thy servant heareth" (1 Samuel 3:10), when he couldn't see the Lord anywhere around with his natural eyes. The nobleman did not know that Jesus could just send His word and the boy would be healed (Psalm 107.20). "Then said Jesus unto him, except ye see signs and wonders, ye will not believe" (John 4:48). The man did not have enough faith in the Word. The nobleman needed a sign and a wonder for his son in order to believe the Word; the centurion needed the Word to see a sign and a wonder for his servant. Jesus had been happy with the faith of the centurion, but not so with the unbelief of the nobleman. The man continued to insist, "Sir, come down ere my child die" (John 4:49). He still needed to see Jesus by his sick son in order to be comforted. He didn't have the faith and humility of the centurion who thought himself unworthy for Christ to come to His house. Jesus had to strengthen the faith of the nobleman since it was weak. Jesus did not go with the man as he had requested but only said, "go thy way; thy son liveth" (John 4:50). The man believed the assuring Word of Jesus, but still his faith level needed to rise. The Bible says, "he went his way. And as he was now going down, his servants met him, and told him, saying, thy son liveth. Then enquired he of them the hour when he began to amend. And they said unto him, yesterday at the seventh hour the fever left him. So the father knew that it was at the same hour, in the which Jesus said unto him, thy son liveth: and himself believed, and his whole house" (John 4:50-53). On his way home, he enquired what time the son had been healed and when he realized it was the same time that Jesus had declared the word of healing, he then believed with his whole house. He knew his son had been healed by the word of Jesus and now had a higher level of faith. If we find that our faith is not what we desire it to be or if we find ourselves plagued by unbelief, we can pray, "help thou mine unbelief" (Mark 9:24). At a point in time, the apostles, "said unto the Lord, increase our faith" (Luke 17:5).

Redemption usually involves - conviction of sin, faith in Christ, then repentance, salvation and grateful worship. The prayer below is a simple prayer of salvation and you can pray this prayer in faith and God will hear you;

Salvation prayer: O Lord, be merciful to me a sinner. I repent of my sins and believe in the name of the Lord Jesus Christ. I receive Him as my personal Lord and Saviour to live with Him forever. Amen

Chapter 4: The Compassion of Jesus brings healing

"O LORD my God, I cried unto thee, and thou hast healed me" (Psalm 30:2).

Jesus healed many, but what motivated Him to do all these healings? He could have refused to accept the deal that God wanted to make with him to be the redeemer of mankind, but He did (John 4.34, John 6.39). He could have stayed up in Heaven with the Father but He came down to dwell amongst us (John 1.14) and to save us like Moses who left the royal palace of Pharaoh to suffer affliction with the Israelites (Hebrews 11.25). He came to give His precious life as God the Son as a ransom for many (Mark 10.45). He knew the law was a heavy yoke and came to give us rest (Matthew 11.28). He came to seek the lost (Luke 19.10). He came to save many (Matthew 18.11). Though He was the Son of God, He came to serve (John 13.1-16). Because of us, He suffered much anguish in Gethsemane and said, "my soul is exceeding sorrowful unto death" (Mark 14:34). He was disgraced, beaten and wounded severely because of our transgressions (Isaiah 53.5). When we felt the heavy weight of our sins, He came to bear them for us (Hebrews 9.28). He assumed a lowly position and humbled Himself to die and be crucified on a tree because of us (Philippians 2.6). In our affliction, He was also afflicted (Isaiah 63.9). Though we deserved judgement, He came to show mercy (Matthew 9.13). We didn't deserve much from Him but he gave us grace (Romans 3.20-24). Though we were guilty, He came to forgive us when we were sinful and evil (Isaiah 43.25). When we were weak, He brought us strength (2 Corinthians 12.8-9). When we were suffering He came to destroy the works of the devil (1 John 3.8). When death was all around us, He came to bring us abundant life (John 10.10). When we were spiritually poor, He came to bring us many riches in Christ Jesus (Ephesians 2.7). Now that you are sick, He wants to bring you healing (Exodus 15.26). He even didn't let the Sabbath days stop him from healing the afflicted and those in bondage (Luke 13.15-16). Why did He go through all this strain to do all these things; because of His love and compassion.

"So He was their Saviour. In all their affliction he was afflicted, and the angel of his presence saved them: in his love and in his pity he redeemed them; and he bare them, and carried them" (Isaiah 63.8-9).

Jesus had much compassion in Him. In fact it was compassion that caused Him to heal the sick; "and Jesus went forth, and saw a great multitude, and was moved with compassion toward them, and He healed their sick" (Matthew 14:14). It was compassion that moved Him to do all that He did for our sakes and lay down His life in His atoning work on the cross. "Greater love hath no man than this, that a man lay down his life for his friends" (John 15:13). He saw the afflicted condition of many; He looked upon their difficulties and struggles; He had pity upon them because it seemed they needed someone who had compassion to care for them. "But when He saw the multitudes, he was moved with compassion on them, because they fainted, and were scattered abroad, as sheep having no shepherd" (Matthew 9:36). It was as though He saw the multitudes as orphans, in need of a father who would attend to them and care for them. He saw them as helpless lambs that needed nursing. "He shall feed His flock like a shepherd: He shall gather the lambs with His arm, and carry them in His bosom, and shall gently lead those that are with young" (Isaiah 40:11). Are you weak and discouraged? Be of good cheer because He is your strength and shield. "Be strong and of a good courage, fear not, nor be afraid of them: for the LORD thy God, He it is that doth go with thee; He will not fail thee, nor forsake thee" (Deuteronomy 31:6). Are you weary and heavy laden, He will give you rest (Matthew 11:28). Have you done something wrong and have repented? Don't worry He will have mercy upon you because, "God, who is rich in mercy, for His great love wherewith He loved us" (Ephesians 2:4). Maybe you did something wrong and it seemed very justified to be punished but can "the lawful captive be delivered? But thus saith the LORD, even the captives of the mighty shall be taken away, and the prey of the terrible shall be delivered: for I will contend with him that contendeth with thee, and I will save thy children" (Isaiah 49:24-25). You might think God has forgotten you or deserted you, but that is very far from the truth; "can a woman forget her sucking child, that she should not have compassion on the son of her womb? Yea, they may forget, yet will I not forget thee" (Isaiah 49:15).

Those who sought healings from Jesus knew the motivating factor driving Him. They knew the mercy and compassion in Him. When the ten lepers saw him, they said unto Him, "have mercy on us" (Luke 17:13). They knew their healing would come about as a result of the mercy that was in Him. In a similar fashion, the Psalmist appeals to the mercy of God for his healing when he says, "have mercy upon me, O LORD; for I am weak: O LORD, heal me; for my bones are vexed" (Psalm 6:2). And so it was with the man whose son was epileptic. The man said to Jesus, "but if thou canst do anything, have compassion on us, and help us" (Mark 9:22). When Jesus had been with his disciples for 3 days and they hadn't had much to eat, He was thoughtful and compassionate, wanting them to eat so they would not faint (Matthew 15:32). When the two blind men saw

Jesus passing by and asked Him for healing, He didn't just touch their eyes, He made sure it was a touch of compassion; "so Jesus had compassion on them, and touched their eyes: and immediately their eyes received sight, and they followed him" (Matthew 20.34). On another occasion, when one leper followed Jesus, seeking healing, Jesus healed him compassionately. Under normal circumstances by Jewish law, a leper was so repulsive that to be close to one, let alone, to touch one would be a huge abomination. But Jesus, "moved with compassion, put forth his hand, and touched him, and saith unto him, I will; be thou clean" (Mark 1:41). When Jesus healed the Gerasene demoniac who had a legion of demons in him, He told him to go home to his friends and tell them how much Jesus had had compassion on him (Mark 5.19). Even, the teaching ministry of Jesus was based on compassion. He "was moved with compassion toward them............and He began to teach them many things" (Mark 6:34). When a woman's only son died and her son's dead body was being carried through town, the woman who was also a widow, was deeply grieved and was crying. Jesus, "had compassion on her, and said unto her, weep not" (Luke 7:13). It's out of His compassion that He wants us to cast our cares upon Him because He cares for us (1st Peter 5.7). For this reason, we must be glad and thankful for the compassion He shows us. Saul said, "blessed be ye of the LORD; for ye have compassion on me" (1st Samuel 23:21).

The following passage is a parable about compassion and forgiveness:

"Therefore is the kingdom of heaven likened unto a certain king, which would take account of his servants. And when he had begun to reckon, one was brought unto him, which owed him ten thousand talents. But forasmuch as he had not to pay, his lord commanded him to be sold, and his wife, and children, and all that he had, and payment to be made. The servant therefore fell down, and worshipped him, saying, Lord, have patience with me, and I will pay thee all. Then the lord of that servant was moved with compassion, and loosed him, and forgave him the debt. But the same servant went out, and found one of his fellowservants, which owed him an hundred pence: and he laid hands on him, and took him by the throat, saying, Pay me that thou owest. And his fellowservant fell down at his feet, and besought him, saying, have patience with me, and I will pay thee all. And he would not: but went and cast him into prison, till he should pay the debt. So when his fellowservants saw what was done, they were very sorry, and came and told unto their lord all that was done. Then his lord, after that he had called him, said unto him, O thou wicked servant, I forgave thee all that debt, because thou desiredst me: shouldest not thou also have had compassion on thy fellowservant, even as I had pity on thee? And his lord was wroth, and delivered him to the tormentors, till he should pay all that was due unto him. So likewise shall my heavenly Father do also unto you, if ye from your hearts forgive not everyone his brother their trespasses" (Matthew 18:23-35).

A certain man owed his master through fraudulent activity - 10,000 talents, to be exact. The master wanted him to be sold, along with his family in order to repay the debt. The man fell down pleading before his master for mercy. The master had compassion and mercy on him and forgave him, cancelling and wiping out all the debt. "Then the lord of that servant was moved with compassion, and loosed him, and forgave him the debt" (Matthew 18.27). This man who had been forgiven also had a servant under him that owed him. It was not as much as 10,000 talents; it was only a hundred pence. But the man, "laid hands on him, and took him by the throat, saying, pay me that thou owest" (Matthew 18.28). Some commentators say the 10,000 talents was equivalent to 2 million pounds; the hundred pence was equivalent to 5 pounds. The man asked him to be patient and to give him time so he would pay back the debt he owed. He did not agree but aggressively sent him to prison. The case was reported to the first master of the unforgiving man. He was shocked and told the man, "o thou wicked servant, I forgave thee all that debt, because thou desiredst me: shouldest not thou also have had compassion on thy fellow-servant, even as I had pity on thee?" The first master made him pay back the 10,000 talents which he owed. Though this man had been shown compassion, he could not do the same for another. The Bible says the way the man was treated by the first master is what the Heavenly Father will do to us if we do not forgive because God forgives us. Our brothers and sisters who offend us owe us five pounds but we owed God 10,000 pounds and He forgave us. Therefore, we should also be able to extend that grace of forgiveness to others. We should be able to forgive 70 x 7 (Matthew 18.22). In this parable, Jesus was showing the compassion He had in the forgiveness of sin. He forgives us because of His compassion.

"And forgive thy people that have sinned against thee, and all their transgressions wherein they have transgressed against thee, and give them compassion before them who carried them captive, that they may have compassion on them" (1st Kings 8:50).
Jesus forgave the sins of the people He healed because of His compassion. Their guilt of sin became a heavy weight on their consciences. No wonder Jesus asked the paralytic the question, "whether is easier, to say, thy sins be forgiven thee; or to say, rise up and walk? (Luke 5:23). Rise up and walk was easier to say. It would take much anguish from being betrayed by His own disciple, Judas, to sweating blood in Gethsemane, to being flogged, to being crucified in order to deal with sin. Moreover, it would only take much compassion to be able to accomplish all these things for man's sake. "Greater love hath no man than this, that a man lay down his life for his friends" (John 15:13). Jesus is grace personified and His grace emanates from His compassion; "and the

LORD was gracious unto them, and had compassion on them, and had respect unto them, because of His covenant with Abraham, Isaac, and Jacob, and would not destroy them, neither cast he them from his presence as yet" (2nd Kings 13:23).

Another way in which Jesus shows His compassion is through the giving of the Holy Spirit. Before Jesus left the earth, He told the disciples that He would send them another Comforter who would come to them. "And I will pray the Father, and He shall give you another Comforter, that he may abide with you forever" (John 14:16). Why did Jesus do this? It was out of compassion. He didn't want His followers to be left alone, not knowing what to do while He was away. He wanted another person, the Holy Spirit, to comfort them. "I will not leave you comfortless: I will come to you" (John 14.18). Furthermore, the Holy Spirit would be a teacher to them. "But the Comforter, which is the Holy Ghost, whom the Father will send in my name, He shall teach you all things" (John 14:26). God cares about us and thus He wants to be with us all the time. Out of compassion, He has sent the Holy Spirit to indwell all believers, so He can be close to us. He does not want to leave you comfortless, He will come to you.

"For every high priest taken from among men is ordained for men in things pertaining to God, that He may offer both gifts and sacrifices for sins: who can have compassion on the ignorant, and on them that are out of the way; for that He himself also is compassed with infirmity" (Hebrews 5:1-2).

When the High priest performed sacrifices for the people, especially on The Day of Atonement, He became their representative. He had mercy and compassion on them because He Himself knew how it felt like to be under the weight of sin. Compassion was a major part of His work. In the same way, Jesus, who is our high priest, knows the weight that sin carries and the toll it can take on us. Therefore, He is compassionate towards us. This is one of the main reasons why He performed the once-and-for-all atonement on the Cross of Calvary. Apart from His atonement, all that He does for us is motivated by compassion. It is because of His love and compassion that He wants to give you abundant life (John 10.10). Jesus' mandate when He came to the earth, outlined in Luke 4.18-19 was a mandate driven by compassion for the multitudes. He went about doing good and healing all that were oppressed of the devil because of His compassion. The gifts of healing work in the church due to His compassion. It was His compassion for the multitudes that made Him wish there were more labourers for the harvest because, "the harvest is truly great but the labourers are few" (Luke 10.2). In fact, the throne of God is referred to as the Mercy Seat. When He comes the second time to rule from His throne in Jerusalem, He would be sitting on the Mercy Seat. Jesus wants to heal you because He is so full of love and mercy. "He healeth the broken in heart, and bindeth up their wounds" (Psalm 147:3). Healing is an act of mercy and His compassion in healing the sick must be published.

"Make you a new heart and a new spirit: for why will ye die, O house of Israel? For I have no pleasure in the death of him that dieth, saith the Lord GOD" (Ezekiel 18:31-32).

In the Scripture above, we can sense God's anguish and longing for His people to make a new heart. Later on in the book of Ezekiel, God again says, "a new heart also will I give you" (Ezekiel 36:26). The yoke of the law was only bringing death to His people. Death here refers to separation from God, which is what happened after Adam ate the forbidden fruit in the Garden of Eden. The people needed the Spirit of God to turn them into new creations (2nd Corinthians 5.17). When God told them to make a new heart, it was virtually impossible for them to accomplish this by themselves - man cannot fix his own heart. Even God does not fix the heart because it's incurably wicked. "The heart is deceitful above all things, and desperately wicked" (Jeremiah 17:9). God always gives a new heart without trying to fix the old (Ezekiel 36.26). Our hearts are our most important stewardship; "keep thy heart with all diligence; for out of it are the issues of life" (Proverbs 4:23). When The Lord was looking for a king to anoint in the house of Jesse, it wasn't about anything apart from the heart. "But the LORD said unto Samuel, look not on his countenance, or on the height of his stature; because I have refused him: for the LORD seeth not as man seeth; for man looketh on the outward appearance, but the LORD looketh on the heart" (1 Samuel 16:7). Yet again God lets us know He wants us to work on our hearts when He says, "whose adorning let it not be that outward adorning of plaiting the hair, and of wearing of gold, or of putting on of apparel; But let it be the hidden man of the heart, in that which is not corruptible, even the ornament of a meek and quiet spirit, which is in the sight of God of great price" (1 Peter 3:3-4).

Furthermore, God points to the heart, encouraging us to have mercy strongly written in them when He says, "let not mercy and truth forsake thee: bind them about thy neck; write them upon the table of thine heart: so shalt thou find favour and good understanding in the sight of God and man" (Proverbs 3:3-4). In following God, we also have to trust Him with our hearts and not lean on our own understanding, in all our ways acknowledging Him so He can make our paths straight (Proverbs 3.5-6). David knew the importance of the heart and that is why He prayed for a clean heart and a right spirit (Psalm 51.10). The Lord also looks at our hearts when He wants to bless us. He urges us saying, "delight thyself also in the LORD; and He shall give thee the desires of thine heart" (Psalm 37:4). The Lord always has His eyes on our hearts, "for the eyes of the LORD run to and fro throughout the whole earth, to shew himself strong on the behalf of them whose heart is perfect toward him" (2 Chronicles 16:9). It is up to us to give our hearts to the Lord because that's our most important stewardship. Let's work on any areas of our lives that are working against us so He can show His benevolence towards us because He wishes to do abundantly more than we expect or can even imagine.

"A new heart also will I give you, and a new spirit will I put within you: and I will take away the stony heart out of your flesh, and I will give you an heart of flesh" (Ezekiel 36:26).
I have assembled below, a few Scriptures that have to do with compassion. You can refer to them to enlighten and refresh your soul on the mercy and compassion of God:

>Psalm 78.38 – "But he, being full of compassion, forgave their iniquity, and destroyed them not: yea, many a time turned he his anger away, and did not stir up all his wrath."
>Psalm 25.10 – "All the paths of the LORD are mercy and truth unto such as keep his covenant and his testimonies."
>Psalm 86.15 – "But thou, O Lord, art a God full of compassion, and gracious, longsuffering, and plenteous in mercy and truth."
>Psalm 111.4 – "He hath made his wonderful works to be remembered: the LORD is gracious and full of compassion."
>Psalm 103.8 – "The LORD is merciful and gracious, slow to anger, and plenteous in mercy."

Psalm 112.4 – "Unto the upright there ariseth light in the darkness: he is gracious, and full of compassion, and righteous."

Psalm 145.8 – "The LORD is gracious, and full of compassion; slow to anger, and of great mercy."

Isaiah 49.15 – "Can a woman forget her sucking child, that she should not have compassion on the son of her womb? yea, they may forget, yet will I not forget thee."

Lam 3.22 – "It is of the LORD'S mercies that we are not consumed, because his compassions fail not."

Lam 3.32 – "But though he cause grief, yet will he have compassion according to the multitude of his mercies."

Micah 7.19 – "He will turn again, he will have compassion upon us; he will subdue our iniquities; and thou wilt cast all their sins into the depths of the sea."

Luke 10.33 - But a certain Samaritan, as he journeyed, came where he was: and when he saw him, he had compassion on him

Luke 15.20 – "And he arose, and came to his father. But when he was yet a great way off, his father saw him, and had compassion, and ran, and fell on his neck, and kissed him."

Romans 9.15 – "For he saith to Moses, I will have mercy on whom I will have mercy, and I will have compassion on whom I will have compassion."

Hebrews 10.34 – "For ye had compassion of me in my bonds, and took joyfully the spoiling of your goods, knowing in yourselves that ye have in heaven a better and an enduring substance."
Jude 22 – "And of some have compassion, making a difference"
1st Pet 3.8 – "Finally, be ye all of one mind, having compassion one of another, love as brethren, be pitiful, be courteous"

Jesus said, "come unto me, all ye that labour and are heavy laden, and I will give you rest. Take my yoke upon you, and learn of me; for I am meek and lowly in heart: and ye shall find rest unto your souls. For my yoke is easy, and my burden is light" (Matthew 11:28-30).

Chapter 5: Different modes of healing

There are various means through which God healed many people through Jesus Christ, the prophets and the apostles in the Bible. This section of the book will take a lot at some of the ways in which God healed people with various afflictions and ailments.

Healing through the Word

Everything we need in life is in the Word. The Word is a source of healing for the wounded body and soul. In the Gospels, there was a man whose request was for Jesus to heal him through His Word only. He knew that God's Word contained power and as a result, asked for healing though the Word. "The centurion answered and said, 'Lord, I am not worthy that You should come under my roof. But only speak a word, and my servant will be healed'" (Mathew 8:8). The centurion knew the power of words; He told Jesus that he would tell a soldier under him to go and he would go and would tell another to come and he would come. The Bible also tells us, "He sent His word and healed them, and delivered them from their destructions" (Psalm 107:20). Healing was accomplished through the Words spoken by God and His Christ. The Bible consists of the Words of God - confessing the parts that speak about healing would bring refreshing healing to your body and soul. The centurion could have asked for some other way of healing, but he specified that healing should come through God's Word.

The Book of Joshua tells us that, "this Book of the Law shall not depart from your mouth, but you shall meditate on it day and night, that you may observe to do according to all that is written in it. For then you will make your way prosperous, and then you will have good success" (Joshua 1:8). Active confession of the Word over and over again can bring healing. One of the ways in which it does this is that it renews the mind and breaks off the deceptions of the devil. Most of the devil's attacks come to the mind first. When the devil came to deceive Eve, he created doubt in her mind about what God had said. That's one of the reasons the helmet of salvation is necessary for Christians. A helmet protects the brain, which is linked with the mind. Being conscious of God's redemption and salvation and confessing the truth of God's Word deals a heavy blow to the devil. Another much-needed weapon is the breastplate of righteousness. We must let the Word of God and the righteousness which Christ imputes to us sink deep in our hearts as we meditate and also confess His Word. "For with the heart one believes unto righteousness, and with the mouth confession is made unto salvation" (Romans 10:10). Confession brings us the benefits of the salvation that God has achieved for us through Christ. We must confess and speak out in faith the Word of God to renew our minds and obtain the benefits of the salvation God has offered us through Christ. "And since we have the same spirit of faith, according to what is written, 'I believed and therefore I spoke,' we also believe and therefore speak" (2nd Corinthians 4:13). It is advisable that we don't leave our minds idle. We need to fill it with positive thoughts as the Scriptures teach us, "whatever things are true, whatever things are noble, whatever things are just, whatever things are pure, whatever things are lovely, whatever things are of good report, if there is any virtue and if there is anything praiseworthy - meditate on these things" (Philippians 4:8).

God wants to heal you. Sickness came into being as a result of man's fall from grace in Genesis 3, but God's redemptive work through the offering of His only begotten Son as a sacrificial lamb, dying on the Cross of Calvary to redeem him from sin and death and becoming a propitiation for our sins (1 John 2.2) provides us with healing. The victory that Christ has won for us must be appropriated by faith as we fight the good fight of faith (1 Timothy 6.12). There have been many Testimonies of people healed of diseases such as cancer and lupus through the confession of the Word. An example is a man named, Jerry Baysinger who is the head pastor of Life Healing ministries. He had terminal cancer but through the confession of the Word, He received healing. You may feel unworthy and might think that Christ shouldn't come to your home at this time to heal you like the Centurion felt, but through His Word, you can be healed.

"My son, give attention to my words; incline your ear to my sayings. Do not let them depart from your eyes; keep them in the midst of your heart; for they are life to those who find them, And health to all their flesh" (Proverbs 4.20-22).

Healing through the laying on of hands

Another method God uses to heal His people is through the laying on of hands.
"Therefore, leaving the discussion of the elementary principles of Christ, let us go on to perfection, not laying again the foundation of repentance from dead works and of faith toward God, of the doctrine of baptisms, of laying on of hands, of resurrection of the dead, and of eternal judgment" (Hebrews 6:1-2).

Laying on of hands is one of the six basic principles of the doctrine of Christ as described in the above verse. They are; repentance, faith toward God, doctrine of baptisms, laying on of hands, resurrection of the dead and eternal judgement. Our focus in this book is the doctrine of the laying on of hands. The laying on of hands was established all the way in the Old Testament. We read, "you shall also have the bull brought before the tabernacle of meeting, and Aaron and his sons shall put their hands on the head of the bull" (Exodus 29:10). Also, we read, "you shall also take one ram, and Aaron and his sons shall put their hands on the head of the ram" (Exodus 29:15). A substitution was taking place here with the laying on of hands on the ram and the bullock. The uprightness of the sacrifices was being exchanged for the deficiencies of Aaron and his sons through faith. Similarly, in the New Testament and in our time, God's healing power can be transferred through Christ to minister to the sick by faith. The laying on of hands is not only for healing but for other functions such as imparting blessing; for authority such as the ordination of ministers or for the infilling of the Spirit as can be seen in the Book of Acts.

Jesus sometimes laid hands on people to heal them. For example, in this passage, He healed some people through the laying on of hands;

"Now He could do no mighty work there, except that He laid His hands on a few sick people and healed them" (Mark 6:5). Jesus was in a town where He wasn't much accepted but through the laying on of hands, He was able to heal a few people who came to Him. Another instance of the use of Jesus' hands in healing is in Mark 7.33-35 where we read, "and he took him aside from the multitude, and put his fingers into his ears, and he spit, and touched his tongue; and looking up to Heaven, he sighed, and saith unto him, Ephphatha, that is, be opened. Immediately his ears were opened, and the impediment of his tongue was loosed, and he spoke plainly" (Mark 7:33-35).

Also in this account, Jesus healed a blind man through the laying on of hands;
"Then He came to Bethsaida; and they brought a blind man to Him, and begged Him to touch him. So He took the blind man by the hand and led him out of the town. And when He had spit on his eyes and put His hands on him, He asked him if he saw anything. And he looked up and said, 'I see men like trees, walking.' Then He put His hands on his eyes again and made him look up. And he was restored and saw everyone clearly. Then He sent him away to his house, saying, 'Neither go into the town, nor tell anyone in the town'" (Mark 8.22-25). Jesus laid hands on him twice as He carried out the healing of the blind man.

On another occasion, Jesus healed a man who was deaf and had a speech impediment through the laying on of hands;
"Then they brought to Him one who was deaf and had an impediment in his speech, and they begged Him to put His hand on him. And He took him aside from the multitude, and put His fingers in his ears, and He spat and touched his tongue. Then, looking up to heaven, He

sighed, and said to him, "ephphatha," that is, 'be opened.' Immediately his ears were opened, and the impediment of his tongue was loosed, and he spoke plainly (Mark 7:32-35).

On another occasion, with regard to the healing of Jairus' daughter, hands were laid for healing by God to be effected;
"And behold, one of the rulers of the synagogue came, Jairus by name. And when he saw Him, he fell at His feet and begged Him earnestly, saying, 'my little daughter lies at the point of death. Come and lay your hands on her, that she may be healed, and she will live.'………. Then He took the child by the hand, and said to her, "talitha, cumi," which is translated, 'little girl, I say to you, arise.' Immediately the girl arose and walked, for she was twelve years of age. And they were overcome with great amazement" (Mark 5.22-23~41-42).

The daughter of Jairus had actually died but Jairus believed that Jesus could turn the situation around. In this account, he asked Jesus not to pray for his daughter but to lay hands on her for her to be healed. The laying on of hands for healing must be received in faith in order for it to work for the recipient.

The apostles also continued the ministry of Jesus and didn't leave out the doctrine of the laying on of hands. "And through the hands of the apostles many signs and wonders were done among the people" (Acts 5.12). Paul was one of the apostles who clearly demonstrated the doctrine of the laying on of hands for healing. In Acts 28.8-9, we read, "and it happened that the father of Publius lay sick of a fever and dysentery. Paul went in to him and prayed, and he laid his hands on him and healed him. So when this was done, the rest of those on the island who had diseases also came and were healed." God, however, makes us know that every believer can practice the doctrine of the laying on of hands for healing. The Bible tells us to, "go into all the world and preach the gospel to every creature............they will lay hands on the sick, and they will recover" (Mark 16.15~18). God has made it possible that believers can lay hands on the sick for them to recover. When hands are laid, God's healing power passes through the hand of the one being used by God to the recipient who must receive the healing by faith. It's not the vessel God is using that does the healing but God Himself; we are to lay hands while God does the healing. The laying on of hands is also a way in which the faith of the recipient is stirred up so he can receive his healing.

Healing through casting out of demons

- Sometimes people were healed when Jesus cast out a demon from them. The demon or a 'spirit of infirmity' was responsible for the malady. After

the demon was cast out, the people received their healing. Consider the passage below;
"As they went out, behold, they brought to Him a man, mute and demon-possessed. And when the demon was cast out, the mute spoke. And the multitudes marveled, saying, 'It was never seen like this in Israel!' (Matthew 9.32-33).
In this case, the man's dumbness was being caused by a demon. When the demon was cast out, the man obtained his healing.

- In another situation, Jesus healed a blind and mute person through the casting out of demons;
"Then one was brought to Him who was demon-possessed, blind and mute; and He healed him, so that the blind and mute man both spoke and saw. And all the multitudes were amazed" (Matthew 12.22-23).
In this situation, we are told that the man was demon-possessed and the demon caused him to be blind and mute. Furthermore, we are told that when he was brought to Jesus, He healed him. The man's healing was as a result of Jesus casting out a demon from him. Luke throws more light on the matter - he says, "and he was casting out a devil, and it was dumb. And it came to pass, when the devil was gone out, the dumb spake; and the people wondered" (Luke 11.14).

- Another Scripture that talks about healing through the casting out of demons can be found in Luke 13.10-13;

"Now He was teaching in one of the synagogues on the Sabbath. And behold, there was a woman who had a

spirit of infirmity eighteen years, and was bent over and could in no way raise herself up. But when Jesus saw her, He called her to Him and said to her, 'woman, you are loosed from your infirmity.' And He laid His hands on her, and immediately she was made straight, and glorified God."

In this situation, the demon is referred to as a spirit of infirmity, which was responsible for placing the body of the woman in a bent position for eighteen years, not giving her the ability to straighten herself up. Jesus spoke a Word of healing and laid hands on her. Consequently, the demon was cast out and the woman was healed.

- Yet another important passage of Scripture can be found in Mark 9.17-27;

"Then one of the crowd answered and said, 'teacher, I brought you my son, who has a mute spirit. And wherever it seizes him, it throws him down; he foams at the mouth, gnashes his teeth, and becomes rigid. So I spoke to your disciples, that they should cast it out, but they could not.' He answered him and said, "o faithless generation, how long shall I be with you? How long shall I bear with you? Bring him to me." Then they brought him to Him. And when he saw Him, immediately the spirit convulsed him, and he fell on the ground and wallowed, foaming at the mouth. So He asked his father, "how long has this been happening to him?" And he said, "from childhood. And often he has thrown him both into the fire and into the water to destroy him. But if you can do anything, have compassion on us and help us." Jesus said to him, "if you can believe, all things are possible to him

who believes."
Immediately the father of the child cried out and said with tears, "Lord, I believe; help my unbelief!" When Jesus saw that the people came running together, He rebuked the unclean spirit, saying to it, "deaf and dumb spirit, I command you, come out of him and enter him no more!" Then the spirit cried out, convulsed him greatly, and came out of him. And he became as one dead, so that many said, 'He is dead.' But Jesus took him by the hand and lifted him up, and he arose."

Many things can be noticed in this passage of Scripture about healing through the casting out of demons. A man brought his son who was mute to Jesus. An evil spirit was causing the boy's condition. The demon was causing him to show very odd and violent symptoms such as foaming at the mouth, the gnashing of teeth and the stiffening of his body. Furthermore, the spirit was causing the boy to have epileptic seizures and was throwing him to the ground. He had suffered this condition for a long time. Jesus' disciples had not been able to cast this demon out and later, when they asked Jesus why they weren't able to do so, He told them that certain demons would only be able to come out through prayer and fasting. The man said to Jesus, "have compassion on us and help us." He was appealing to the compassion that Jesus had in order for his child to be healed. Jesus was indeed touched by the man's situation and told him that if he could believe, all things would be possible. The man said something very interesting - he said, Lord, "I believe; help my unbelief." He was expressing humility in this statement. He knew that even for him to believe, He would need the help of the Saviour. It was as though he knew John 15.5, "I am the vine, you are the branches. He who abides in me, and I in him, bears much fruit; for without Me you can do nothing." Jesus spoke to the spirit, commanding it to come out of him and though the spirit caused the boy to have further convulsions, it finally came out. After the episode, the boy seemed as though he was dead, but Jesus touched him and lifted him up. As a result, the boy was back to good health again. The boy achieved His healing when Jesus cast out a devil from him.

- A very remarkable healing is also described in the Bible in Mark 5.1-13. It is about a man who was possessed by a very terrible demon;

"Then they came to the other side of the sea, to the country of the Gadarenes. And when he had come out of the boat, immediately there met Him out of the tombs a man with an unclean spirit, who had his dwelling among the tombs; and no one could bind him, not even with chains, because he had often been bound with shackles and chains. And the chains had been pulled apart by him, and the shackles broken in pieces; neither could anyone tame him. And always, night and day, he was in the mountains and in the tombs, crying out and cutting himself with stones. When he saw Jesus from afar, he ran and worshiped Him. And he cried out with a loud voice and said, "What have I to do with You, Jesus, Son of the Most High God? I implore you by God that You do not torment me." For He said to him, 'Come out of the man, unclean spirit!' Then He asked him, 'what is your name?' And he answered, saying, "my name is Legion;

for we are many." Also he begged Him earnestly that He would not send them out of the country. Now a large herd of swine was feeding there near the mountains. So all the demons begged Him, saying, "send us to the swine, that we may enter them." And at once Jesus gave them permission. Then the unclean spirits went out and entered the swine (there were about two thousand); and the herd ran violently down the steep place into the sea, and drowned in the sea."

Several things about demons and about healing can be noticed in this passage of Scripture. Jesus and His disciples had been on a boat in the sea, crossing over to the other side. When they got to the other side of the sea, they were faced with a very disturbing situation – a demon-possessed man living in tombs. The demons had tortured him so much and had made him live in filthy environments - in tombs. The demons had also given him abnormal strength, making him so aggressive that he could not be bound with chains, but could break them apart. The demon realized the person and authority of Jesus Christ and asked Him not to torment him. Jesus commanded the unclean spirit to come out. He also asked for its name. The demon replied and said, 'my name is Legion; for we are many.' The name 'legion,' which means 'thousands,' is a word taken from a Latin term for a large group of soldiers. The term is used by the Holy Spirit here to indicate that the man was not only being possessed by a large number of demons, but specifically, by a large number of demonic military troops, connoting that the demons were a force to reckon with. The number of soldiers in a Roman legion, which was the largest unit of the Roman army, differed from time to time, involving about 3000 men in early times, but increasing to about 5,500 men in later times. The demons begged Jesus not to allow them to be sent outside the country but rather, into a large herd of swine that were feeding close-by. The Bible tells us that about 2000 demons were cast into the swine and caused them to ran violently into the sea. The people that had been taking care of the swine went and informed others about what had happened. When people in the town came and saw the man that had been demon-possessed, we are told that, "then they came to Jesus, and saw the one who had been demon-possessed and had the legion, sitting and clothed and in his right mind" (Mark 5.15). The man had been healed through the casting out of demons from him. The demons not only caused him physical distress, but mental distress as well, but now he was 'in his right mind.' When Jesus was leaving, the man wanted to leave with him but Jesus told him, "go home to your friends, and tell them what great things the Lord has done for you, and how He has had compassion on you" (Mark 5.19). Here, we see that Jesus wanted the testimony of this healing to be broadcast. It should be noted that on some other occasions, however, Jesus told the people He healed not to tell of it except telling only the priest (Matthew 8.4). Jesus dealt with different situations in a unique manner. Also we see the compassion of Jesus at work again – indeed, it was His compassion that stirred Him to heal the man.

- In Luke 4.35-37, we are presented with another account of a healing performed by Jesus through the casting out of a demon.

"Then He went down to Capernaum, a city of Galilee, and was teaching them on the Sabbaths. And they were astonished at His teaching, for His word was with authority. Now in the synagogue there was a man who had a spirit of an unclean demon. And he cried out with a loud voice, saying, 'let us alone! What have we to do with you, Jesus of Nazareth? Did you come to destroy us? I know who you are—the Holy One of God!' But Jesus rebuked him, saying, "be quiet, and come out of him!" And when the demon had thrown him in their midst, it came out of him and did not hurt him. Then they were all amazed and spoke among themselves, saying, 'what a word this is! For with authority and power He commands the unclean spirits, and they come out. And the report about Him went out into every place in the surrounding region."

In this account, Jesus was teaching in a synagogue. There was a man in the congregation who had unclean spirits in him. This shows us that unclean spirits can still afflict those who attend church services. The spirits in the man called out to Jesus, recognizing His authority and asking Him to leave them alone. Jesus spoke to the demon, telling it to come out of the man. The demon threw the man into the crowd and then came out of him. The people around were amazed at the power of Jesus.

Throughout Jesus' ministry on earth, He showed compassion upon people by healing them through the casting out of demons. He did this for many people (See

Mark 1.34, Luke 4.41, Mark 1.39). When demons are cast out and we get healed, we should get closer to Jesus, who healed us. The Bible tells us that after Jesus had resurrected, He went first to Mary Magdalene out of which He had cast out 7 demons (Mark 16.9). Mary Magdalene had gotten closer to Jesus after getting her healing from Him. Healing forms a part of God's redemptive work through Christ. God has made it possible for an exchange to take place between Jesus, who has perfect health and us, who are the descendants of Adam, who through disobedience and the original sin, sin and sickness got the opportunity to afflict us all (Romans 5). "When evening had come, they brought to Him many who were demon-possessed. And He cast out the spirits with a word, and healed all who were sick, that it might be fulfilled which was spoken by Isaiah the prophet, saying: "He Himself took our infirmities and bore our sicknesses" (Matthew 8.16-17). Another reason why it is essential for people who receive healing from God to get closer to Him can be found in the Scriptures, specifically in Luke 11.24-26. "When an unclean spirit goes out of a man, he goes through dry places, seeking rest; and finding none, he says, 'I will return to my house from which I came.' And when he comes, he finds it swept and put in order. Then he goes and takes with him seven other spirits more wicked than himself, and they enter and dwell there; and the last state of that man is worse than the first" (Luke 11.24-26).

When an unclean spirit is cast out of a person and he does not put on the armour of God (Ephesians 6) and does not fellowship closely with Jesus Christ, the spirits can return and cause even more havoc than they did before they were cast out. It is always essential that we continue to conduct spiritual warfare as Paul informed us in the sixth chapter of the epistle to the Ephesians. It is also essential that we work to develop a closer fellowship with the Lord Jesus Christ. "But if we walk in the light, as he is in the light, we have fellowship one with another, and the blood of Jesus Christ his Son cleanseth us from all sin" (1st John 1.6-8).

Sometimes people get the impression that they can receive healing from 'mediums' who conduct healing through spirits other than God. Such people are deceiving themselves as well as their patients. Jesus said, "every kingdom divided against itself is brought to desolation, and every city or house divided against itself will not stand. If satan casts out satan, he is divided against himself. How then will his kingdom stand?" (Matthew 12.26-28). Satan cannot cast out satan. It takes a higher power, which is the power of God in Jesus to cast out satan and his demons. Most of these false healers only transfer the ailment from one part of the body to another. For example, if someone has a pain in the shoulder and goes for healing from a witch doctor, the witch doctor might inconspicuously just transfer the ailment from the shoulder to the knee. When the knee starts developing issues, the patient wouldn't know that this 'transfer' took place at the witch doctors' shrine.

Jesus is the only genuine healer who healed then and still heals now.

"On that very day some Pharisees came, saying to Him, "get out and depart from here, for Herod wants to kill you." And He said to them, "go, tell that fox, 'behold, I cast out demons and perform cures today and tomorrow, and the third day I shall be perfected" (Luke 13.31-32).

Healing through touch

On some few occasions, the Bible informs us of Jesus' healing through touch. For example, Mathew 8.14 gives us an instance of this;

- "Now when Jesus had come into Peter's house, He saw his wife's mother lying sick with a fever. So He touched her hand, and the fever left her. And she arose and served them" (Matthew 8.14).
  Jesus came to Peter's house and saw that his mother had gotten ill with a fever. Jesus touched her hand and she received healing.

- Another instance of healing through the compassionate touch of Jesus can be found in Matthew 8.1-3;
  When He had come down from the mountain, great multitudes followed Him. And behold, a leper came and worshiped Him, saying, 'Lord, if You are willing, You can make me clean.'
  Then Jesus put out His hand and touched him,

saying, 'I am willing; be cleansed.' Immediately his leprosy was cleansed" (Matthew 8.1-3).
Here, Jesus healed a man with leprosy through touch. The man showed humility to Jesus when he asked Him that if He was willing, He could make him clean. Jesus compassionately told him that He was willing and healed the man. Mark captures this when he says, "then Jesus, moved with compassion, stretched out His hand and touched him, and said to him, 'I am willing; be cleansed'" (Mark 1.41).

- Jesus healed a man through touch in Mark 7.33
"Again, departing from the region of Tyre and Sidon, He came through the midst of the region of Decapolis to the Sea of Galilee. Then they brought to Him one who was deaf and had an impediment in his speech, and they begged Him to put His hand on him. And He took him aside from the multitude, and put His fingers in his ears, and He spat and touched his tongue. Then, looking up to Heaven, He sighed, and said to him, 'ephphatha,' that is, 'be opened.'"
In this case, a man who was deaf and had a speech impediment was brought to Jesus. Jesus healed him through touching his tongue and his ears and speaking a Word of healing.

- Matthew 20.29-34 also presents us of an account in the Bible where Jesus healed 2 blind men through touch.
"Now as they went out of Jericho, a great multitude followed Him. And behold, two blind men sitting by the road, when they heard that Jesus was passing by, cried out, saying, 'have mercy on us, O Lord, Son of David!' Then the multitude warned them that they

should be quiet; but they cried out all the more, saying, 'have mercy on us, O Lord, Son of David!' So Jesus stood still and called them, and said, 'what do you want Me to do for you?' They said to Him, 'Lord, that our eyes may be opened.' So Jesus had compassion and touched their eyes. And immediately their eyes received sight, and they followed Him."
Jesus was leaving Jericho when He met 2 blind men sitting by the road. They asked Jesus for mercy, knowing that He was full of compassion. Jesus responded to them asking what He could do for them. They responded by requesting that their eyes be opened. Jesus touched their eyes and they received their sight.

- In another instance, Jesus healed the ear of a man who had come to oppose Him;
"When those around Him saw what was going to happen, they said to Him, 'Lord, shall we strike with the sword?' And one of them struck the servant of the high priest and cut off his right ear. But Jesus answered and said, 'Permit even this.' And He touched his ear and healed him." (Luke 22.51)
During the last days of Jesus' ministry on the earth, when He was betrayed by Judas, a confrontation developed between the disciples of Jesus on the one hand and Judas, the chief priest, captains of the temple, the elders and some guards on the other. Peter then took a knife and cut off the ear of one of the servants of the chief priest. But Jesus compassionately touched the ear of the servant and it was restored.

On other occasions Jesus' people received their healing not through being touched by Him, but rather, they touching Jesus

- An instance can be found in Matthew 9.20-22. "And suddenly, a woman who had a flow of blood for twelve years came from behind and touched the hem of His garment. For she said to herself, 'if only I may touch His garment, I shall be made well.' But Jesus turned around, and when He saw her He said, 'Be of good cheer, daughter; your faith has made you well.' And the woman was made well from that hour." The woman with the issue of blood had the faith that even if she touched the hem of Christ's garment, she would be healed. It worked and she received her healing. Jesus told her that her faith had made her well. The hem of the garment in those days was a representation of the authority of the person who wore it. Jesus had the authority to heal and that's what he did. Also, in Luke 6.17-19, again many people were healed when they touched Jesus.

  "And He came down with them and stood on a level place with a crowd of His disciples and a great multitude of people from all Judea and Jerusalem, and from the seacoast of Tyre and Sidon, who came to hear Him and be healed of their diseases, as well as those who were tormented with unclean spirits. And they were healed. And the whole multitude sought to touch Him, for power went out from Him and healed them all" (Luke 6.17-19).

  Jesus was preaching in a town when many people came to hear him. He healed many who were being oppressed by demons and many that were sick. One of the ways through which the people here received their healing was through touching Jesus.

- In another instance in the Bible, many people received their healing through touching Jesus. "When they had crossed over, they came to the land of Gennesaret and anchored there. And when they came out of the boat, immediately the people recognized Him, ran through that whole surrounding region, and began to carry about on beds those who were sick to wherever they heard He was. Wherever He entered, into villages, cities, or the country, they laid the sick in the marketplaces, and begged Him that they might just touch the hem of His garment. And as many as touched Him were made well" (Mark 6.53-56).

Jesus and His disciples had sailed to another part of town called Gennesaret, located on the Northwest shore of the Sea of Galilee in Israel. Many people saw Jesus and ran to him. They carried many who were sick to Him so He would heal them. The people begged Him to allow the sick to touch the hem of His garment so that they would be healed. Jesus allowed this and as a result, the sick received their healing from touching the hem of His garment. Another interesting thing to note is this part of the passage above; 'wherever He entered, into villages, cities, or the country, they laid the sick in the marketplaces.' Jesus was not only conducting healings in Synagogues but in the cities, villages and marketplaces.

Healing through the anointing oil

Oil, in ancient times was used as a healing agent to comfort and clean wounds (Isaiah 1.6). We see that this practice was continued in the time of the early church (Luke 10.34). Luke in particular would capture such an event in his book because he was a physician. But at other times, the oil was not used as a healing agent in and of itself but would serve as a symbol of the Holy Spirit as well as a symbolic item that would inspire faith in the patient and cause God to bring healing supernaturally. Such an event occurred in Mark 6.13; "and they cast out many devils, and anointed with oil many that were sick, and healed them" (Mark 6:13). Earlier in the chapter, Jesus gave the twelve disciples authority over unclean spirits and then later sent them out. What really caused the healing was the authority that Jesus had given them to cast out devils and heal the sick through the power of the Holy Spirit and not the oil itself. The oil here was serving as a symbol of the Holy Spirit (Zechariah 4.4-6). Furthermore, the anointing oil in this case and in our usage today serves as a symbolic reminder of the supernatural healing authority and power of the Holy Spirit (Acts 10.38). The healing was done by the Spirit of God and not the one administering the anointing oil.

In a church congregation, if one is sick, he can inform the elders of the church who would come and pray for him in Jesus' name and would anoint him with oil.
"Is anyone among you sick? Let him call for the elders of the church, and let them pray over him, anointing him with oil in the name of the Lord" (James 5:14).
Some people are not able to stand on 1st Peter 2.24 which shows that by the stripes of God they were healed. They may need people with higher levels of faith to assist them to attain their healing and that's ok. Such ailing Christians need to be cared for. God loves all and has made provision for everyone in the church to be able to receive healing. Therefore, if you are sick, there is no problem in calling for the elders of the church to minister to you.

Healing through the gifts of healings

"To another gifts of healings by the same Spirit" (1 Corinthians 12:9).

The gifts of healings fall under one of the 3 categories of spiritual gifts being the vocal gifts, the power gifts and the revelation gifts. The gifts of healings are classified under power gifts.

Though some believe that the gifts of healing have ceased to exist, this is not true - they still exist and are functioning in the church today. Also notice, the verse says, 'gifts of healing.' This points us to the fact that the gifts of healing come in many different manifestations. Each time a healing occurs, it is a gift given through the person by whom the gift is manifested. "But the manifestation of the Spirit is given to each one for the profit of all" (1st Corinthians 12.7). It also points to the fact that the gifts of healing manifest differently based on the ailment being addressed. Certain kinds of ailments would let a specific gift of the gifts of healing to address that problem. No wonder Jesus said, "howbeit, this kind goeth not out but by prayer and fasting" (Matthew 17.21). The gifts of healings are also under God's control, so you can't just enter a hospital and start healing everyone there if God has not willed it. An instance of the gifts of healing can be found in this passage;

"Now there is in Jerusalem by the Sheep Gate a pool, which is called in Hebrew, Bethesda, having five porches. In these lay a great multitude of sick people, blind, lame, paralyzed, waiting for the moving of the water.............Now a certain man was there who had an infirmity thirty-eight years. When Jesus saw him lying there, and knew that he already had been in that condition a long time, He said to him, 'Do you want to be made well?' The sick man answered Him, 'Sir, I have no man to put me into the pool when the water is stirred up; but while I am coming, another steps down before me.' Jesus said to him, 'Rise, take up your bed and walk.' And immediately the man was made well, took up his bed, and walked" (John 5.2-3,5-9).

In this instance, Jesus healed a man who had been bedridden by the Pool of Bethesda for 38 years. When Jesus got there, He healed only that man though there were many other people there who had been sick for a while. The gifts of healing operated through Jesus to heal this man in question, under God's sovereign will and control. When Jesus was done with this one healing that God had done through Him, he left. Similarly, in a particular church service, those people that God has appointed to be healed at that time would be the ones that God would heal through the minister operating with the gifts of healing.

Sometimes the gifts of healing will operate in one person but would consequently cause other people to be healed as well. Such an example can be found in Acts 28.7-9;

"In that region there was an estate of the leading citizen of the island, whose name was Publius, who received us and entertained us courteously for three days. And it happened that the father of Publius lay sick of a fever and dysentery. Paul went in to him and prayed, and he laid his hands on him and healed him. So when this was done, the rest of those on the island who had diseases also came and were healed. They also honored us in many ways; and when we departed, they provided such things as were necessary."

The healing of this one man caught the attention of many others and increased their faith, making them able to receive healing as well. Such healings also create an atmosphere for belief and draw people's attention to the Gospel.

The gifts of healing can be said to be a supernatural manifestation of the healing ability by the Holy Spirit through one individual to another. It is mentioned in 1st Corinthians 12.9 and operates according to God's sovereign will and that's why at a point in time Miletus had to be left sick (2 Timothy 4.20). Sometimes God heals slowly and according to His own timing.

Healing through communion

One of the best ways of healing by the Lord is through the taking of communion. There have been many testimonies of people being healed through the taking of communion. The wine of the communion represents the blood of the Lord, which forgives our sin whilst the bread represents His body, which refreshes our bodies. So taking communion is a double-edged sword – we receive forgiveness for our spirits through the blood and revitalizing of our bodies with His body. Ailments such as headaches, diabetes, cancers, eye disorders and more have been healed through the taking of communion. Sometimes healing takes place progressively and some ministers let the sick take communion thrice a day as though they were taking medicine. The faith of these

Christians builds up to receive their healing as they take the communion continually. Special bread or wine is not required because it is your faith that brings about the healing. It is also important to meditate on the reality of the wounds and stripes on the body of Jesus bringing us healing. Moreover, meditate on the fact that He has exchanged your diseases for His health. By breaking the bread, we remember the breaking of His body for our sakes so we may attain healing. Faith is a key aspect of healing through communion. "What things soever ye desire, when ye pray, believe that ye receive them, and ye shall have them" (Mathew 11.24).

Some Healing ministers

William Branham

William Marrion Branham, commonly known as William Branham was born on 6th April 1909 into a poor family in Kentucky. When he was young, he heard a voice telling him not to drink, smoke or defile his body in any way because he would have spiritual work to do when he got older. William struggled with God in his youthful days but began to seek Him more and more as time went by. He sought God most fervently when he became sick and thought he would die. While sick on the hospital bed, he heard the same voice that spoke to him in his youth telling him that he had been called and would not go. Branham replied saying if he was allowed to live, he would preach the gospel. He felt better and then sought a church where he could repent and be discipled. He found one in which he was prayed for and he received his healing as well. He also sought the Baptism of the Spirit and received it. His zeal was kindled and he began to hold many meetings. God also began to use him as prophet, giving him many visions of events that would occur. At one time, he received a visitation from an angel that told him that he was a seer prophet and gave him two signs; first he would see sicknesses in people and secondly, he would be able to see sins in their life from which they had to repent. His healing ministry began from this point. Not only did he minister in the United States, but he also ministered internationally. Many deaf, blind, dumb and crippled people were healed through his ministry.

Oral Roberts

Granville Oral Roberts, commonly known as Oral Roberts, was born in Oklahoma on January 24th, 1918. His father was a preacher who established a number of Pentecostal churches in addition to his occupation as a farmer. His mother was also a deeply religious Christian who prayed for the sick. She dedicated Oral Roberts to God's service when she was pregnant with the young Oral in her womb. There was one problem, however; Oral was a strong stutterer. His mum kept telling him that one day, God would heal him and he would minister to crowds – and that is exactly what happened. In his youthful days, Oral departed from the Christian foundations that had been laid for him by his family and began to live a wild life. He soon began to experience health problems and was diagnosed with tuberculosis, which made him lose a lot of weight. Oral turned backed to God within this dark period. God told his elder sister that He was going to heal him and momentarily, a travelling evangelist called George Moncey came to town. Oral's brother decided to take him to one of George Moncey's meetings and Oral received his healing immediately. It so happened that on his way to this meeting, God had already spoken to Oral, telling him that He was going to heal him and that he was going to take God's healing power to his generation. Oral became a travelling evangelist within America as well as overseas, with the healing grace to heal the sick. He also made very good use of the media and people who watched television and saw others being healed and receiving Christ. Many were healed and many souls were saved by God through him, with the operation of the gift of healings.

Smith Wigglesworth

Smith Wigglesworth was a British evangelist born on 8th June 1859. He was born to a poor family that did not believe in God, unfortunately. Smith, however, desired to know God. He prayed in his youth and his grandmother, who was a stonge Christian took him to church meetings. He committed himself to the Lord in one of these meetings when He got to know about the love of God. He also began to fast frequently while praying for souls. Smith worked as a plumber besides doing the work of the ministry. He delighted to care for the youth and destitute children by feeding them and inviting them for meetings. Many got saved during these meetings

One day, Smith heard of a healing meeting that was going to take place in town. His wife, Polly was sick and he took her there. She received her healing in this meeting. Smith, who initially did not embrace the reality of healing now began to look to God for healing, since he was also sick. He also got his healing. Furthermore, one time when two of his children got sick, he and his wife prayed for them and they also got healed instantly. Soon, he began to hold meetings where many people would come and get healed. The blind saw; the deaf heard; the crippled walked. The Holy Spirit began to use him mightily and many people were saved through his ministry.

Alexander Dowie

John Alexander Dowie was born in Scotland in May 1847. He, as well as his family, however, moved to Australia where he spent a considerable portion of his life. His father was a tailor who also preached the gospel. He decided that he wanted to enter the ministry and consequently enrolled in a University to study. Afterwards, he became a pastor of a church. God soon revealed to him that divine healing was for today. He began to move in the healing grace of the Holy Spirit as he began to pray for people, who received their healing. Soon, he became a full-time healing evangelist. He held many meetings in which people received spectacular healings from God. He also published journals on healing and his congregation fed the poor, carrying out evangelism as well. The Holy Spirit healed many people through his ministry. As a result, many came to the knowledge of Jesus Christ. The gifts of healings are for the modern day church and God still heals people with these gifts today.

Healing through the gift of faith

The 'gift of faith' is one of the 9 gifts of the Spirit. This gift is different from the normal faith we talk about in Christianity, which is defined in Hebrews 11.1. The gift of faith can be seen in Acts 14.8-5 when Paul healed the crippled man at Lystra. Paul, with the gift of faith, "said with a loud voice, stand upright on thy feet. And he leaped and walked" (Acts 14:10). The operation of the gift is also seen in Acts 3.2-9, when Peter with the gift of faith operating in him by the power of the Holy Spirit said to the crippled man, "silver and gold have I none; but such as I have give I thee: in the name of Jesus Christ of Nazareth rise up and walk. And he took him by the right hand, and lifted him up: and immediately his feet and ankle bones received strength" (Act 3:6-7).

Healing through prayer

"Again I say unto you, that if two of you shall agree on earth as touching anything that they shall ask, it shall be

done for them of my Father which is in heaven" (Matthew 18:19).

This also means that when two Christians meet and pray for healing in agreement, the healing will be granted in Jesus' name. Remember, this is a prayer of agreement and unity. It is not a church meeting prayer, but one offered between two Christians in agreement. When this is done, God will watch over His Word and release healing. It could be two friends, relatives or a married couple. It is not necessary to bring in a thousand people for this prayer because the scripture says, "if two of you shall agree on earth as touching anything that they shall ask, it shall be done for them of my Father which is in Heaven. For where two or three are gathered together in my name, there am I in the midst of them" (Matthew 18:19-20). Even when two people are gathered and are praying, God is there with them. Two are enough for the healing. If two agree, it shall be done.

A sick person can also pray for himself; "therefore I say unto you, what things soever ye desire, when ye pray, believe that ye receive them, and ye shall have them" (Mark 11:24). If you are sick, pray and believe that you would get healed and you will. Sometimes you may still feel the symptoms and you may not feel different but continue to believe that you are healed, reminding yourself of 1st Peter 2.24 which says, "by whose stripes ye were healed" (1st Peter 2:24). Faith is not about feeling, it is about knowing. When you believe, you receive.

Healing through direction

Sometimes God heals through giving a direction to be followed. When that direction is observed, healing results. This kind of healing can be found in the life of Naaman the Syrian in the Book of 2nd Kings;

"Now Naaman, commander of the army of the king of Syria, was a great and honorable man in the eyes of his master, because by him the Lord had given victory to Syria. He was also a mighty man of valor, but a leper...........So it was, when Elisha the man of God heard that the king of Israel had torn his clothes, that he sent to the king, saying, 'please let him come to me, and he shall know that there is a prophet in Israel.' Then Naaman went with his horses and chariot, and he stood at the door of Elisha's house. And Elisha sent a messenger to him, saying, 'Go and wash in the Jordan seven times, and your flesh shall be restored to you, and you shall be clean.' But Naaman became furious, and went away and said, 'indeed, I said to myself, He will surely come out to me, and stand and call on the name of the Lord his God, and wave his hand over the place, and heal the leprosy.' Are not the Abanah and the Pharpar, the rivers of Damascus, better than all the waters of Israel? Could I not wash in them and be clean?' So he turned and went away in a rage. And his servants came near and spoke to him, and said, 'my father, if the prophet had told you to do something great, would you not have done it? How much more then, when he says to you, 'wash, and be clean'?' So he went down and dipped seven times in the Jordan, according to the saying of the man of God; and his flesh was restored like the flesh of a little child, and he was clean. And he returned to the man of God, he and all his aides, and came and stood before him; and he said, 'Indeed, now I know that there is no God in all the earth, except in Israel.'" (2nd Kings 5.1-15)

Naaman was a very good commander of the Syrian army and his superiors held him in high esteem because God favoured him and gave him victories in many battles. There was one problem, however, Naaman was a leper. His wife got information from a servant girl from Israel who said that a prophet in Israel would be able to heal him. Naaman informs his superiors and he goes to Israel with a letter to the king. The king of Israel was not in a position to help but Elisha the prophet could have sent a message to the king of Israel so he would allow Naaman to come and see him. When Naaman got to Elisha's house, Elisha didn't even give him the courtesy of coming out to see him (this, however, should not be interpreted to mean that prophets should not be courteous. It could be that in this instance, God specifically directed him to act in this way. Furthermore, Old Testament prophets were usually more stern).

Elisha sent a messenger to him with the following message, "go and wash in the Jordan seven times, and your flesh shall be restored to you, and you shall be clean." Naaman was infuriated by this message because he was thinking Elisha would come out and see him and pray for him. The river that Elisha had asked him to wash in didn't seem appealing. He considered the rivers of Syria, more refreshing than those of Israel. He almost left, but his servant asked him to reconsider and heed to Elisha's directives, adding that the instruction is not too difficult to follow. Sometimes our pride and impatience can get in the way of God's blessings. When Elisha finally followed the instructions of the prophets, he was healed and gave glory to God. He had been healed by following directives given to him by God through the prophet. It should be added that the Bible advises us to "test the spirits, whether they are of God; because many false prophets have gone out into the world" (1st John 4.1). Likewise, when Jesus anointed the blind man's eyes with clay and sent him to wash away the clay in the Pool of Siloam, the man obeyed and received his sight (John 9.6-12). Had he not obeyed the directions for healing, his healing would not have come about.

Healing through fasting

"Is not this the fast that I have chosen? To loose the bands of wickedness, to undo the heavy burdens, and to let the oppressed go free, and that ye break every yoke?.....Then shall thy light break forth as the morning, and thine health shall spring forth speedily: and thy righteousness shall go before thee; the glory of the LORD shall be thy rereward" (Isaiah 58:6,8).

This Scripture in Isaiah is one of the best Scriptures on fasting. Don't get me wrong; every Scripture in the Bible about fasting is wonderful of course. This passage can be entitled as 'God's chosen fast'. Such a fast loosens the bands of wickedness and undoes the heavy burdens in your life. It also breaks yokes off your life. Furthermore, it brightens up your life and causes speedy healing. When the healing results, God gets the glory.

There was a testimony of a man who had an autoimmune disorder that affected his joints and liver. He went to the most expensive hospitals in his locality in search of healing and took all the drugs he could take but nothing helped. This made him very agitated and distressed. He heard of a prayer meeting and decided to attend. He embarked on a fasting program for a number of days. As he began to fast, within a few number of days he received his healing. Consequently, he was overjoyed and testified about the mercy and grace of the Lord.

Another patient suffered from a mouth injury, which caused him to have excruciating pain in his mouth especially when he ate food. He often wept in pain. After some time, he decided to listen to testimonies of how God had healed others of their diseases. He decided to fast for a number of days, confessing his sins and seeking to have an encounter with the Lord. After just a few days, he noticed that the damaged tissues inside his mouth were tearing away and the pain was disappearing. He got completely healed as he continued to fast and gave glory to the Lord. There are certain conditions and situations in life that respond very well to fasting and prayer. "Howbeit this kind goeth not out but by prayer and fasting" (Mathew 17.21).

Healing through Mantles, Handkerchiefs etc.

"Now God worked unusual miracles by the hands of Paul, so that even handkerchiefs or aprons were brought from his body to the sick, and the diseases left them and the evil spirits went out of them" (Acts 19.11-12).
A healing brings relief from disease or injury, but cannot be easily perceived by spectators with the senses. It may also not be instant but rather gradual. A miracle, on the other hand, can usually be perceived with the senses and is almost instant – it's usually more intense than a healing. For example, when a person who has one limb shorter than the other gets a miracle whereby the short

limb is visibly lengthened, this may be considered as being more of a miracle than a healing. But a healing and a miracle can overlap with each another. For example, Derek Prince spoke about once praying for a certain lady who had acne and wasn't expecting to see anything spectacular, but within the next few minutes, the lady's face started glowing with a pink color. Now this was spectacular; the healing was miraculous. God used Paul to perform miracles, which included miraculous healings. The power of God through the Holy Spirit was passed from Paul to the sick and demon-oppressed through items such as handkerchiefs and aprons.

Healing through the name of Jesus

The name of Jesus is the most powerful name in the universe. "That at the name of Jesus every knee should bow, of things in heaven, and things in earth, and things under the earth" (Philippians 2:10). Jesus entreats us to ask for things he has promised us in His Word such as healings in His name. "And whatsoever ye shall ask in my name, that will I do, that the Father may be glorified in the Son" (John 14:13). The Holy Spirit working with the Apostles performed healings when they used the name of Jesus. Peter and Paul, on some occasions commanded crippled people to rise up and walk in the name of Jesus. We can demand healing from God because He has promised it to us in His Word. When you do this in His name, you are demanding for something that Jesus has promised to give you. In my name they shall lay hands on the sick, and they shall recover" (Mark 16:17,18). According to Colossians 2.15, Jesus has defeated evil forces opposing Him and the church. As a result, He has made many blessings available to us, including the blessing of healing. Besides, Jesus repeated in John 14.14, "if ye shall ask any thing in my name, I will do it" (John 14:14). Again, Jesus repeats this when He said, "verily, verily, I say unto you, whatsoever ye shall ask the Father in my name, He will give it you. Hitherto have ye asked nothing in my name: ask, and ye shall receive, that your joy may be full" (John 16:23-24). Jesus was teaching them that whatever they ask in His name will be granted and that until then, they hadn't asked Him for anything. He entreats them to ask so they would receive, which would make them joyful. The name of Jesus is a gateway to numerous blessings that God has for us. In His name, we have deliverance, healing and many other blessings. It's not about any other name but the name of Jesus, the Son of God. Peter said at one time, "why marvel ye at this? Or why look ye so earnestly on us, as though by our own power or holiness we had made this man to walk?" (Acts 3:12). Peter knew that the miracle at the Gate called Beautiful was not by His own power or strength but one that could have only been accomplished in the name of Jesus. "And his name through faith in his name hath made this man strong, whom ye see and know: yea, the faith which is by him hath given him this perfect soundness in the presence of you all" (Acts 3:16).

When Jesus sent out the seventy which he had appointed to proclaim His kingdom, He told them "heal the sick there, and say to them, 'the kingdom of God has come near to you'" (Luke 10:9). When they did so and came back to Jesus, they reported, "Lord, even the demons are subject to us in Your name" (Luke 10.17). Philip was able to catch up with the Ethiopian eunuch's chariot and taught Him about Jesus from the Book of Isaiah. Some say that when the eunuch returned to Ethiopia, many people there turned to Christianity. Philip's focus had been Jesus and His wonderful name and it made all the difference in Ethiopia.

Healing Through medicine

"No longer drink only water, but use a little wine for your stomach's sake and your frequent infirmities" (1 Timothy 5:23).

By the use of wine in this Scripture, I am not indicating that people should use wine as a cure for their ailments but rather to indicate that apart from divine healing, sometimes healing can and does take place through the administration of medicine to the patient. I use wine here to refer to medicine, because this was the motive of the apostle when he spoke about this to Timothy.

Timothy was not one given to the recreational drinking of wine, otherwise the apostle would not have urged him to use it as medicine. We therefore learn from this Scripture that apart from divine methods, sometimes a little medicine can be administered to cure certain ailments. If, for example, one has a cough, a little cough mixture may help ease the condition.

"Is there no balm in Gilead, is there no physician there? Why then is there no recovery for the health of the daughter of my people?" (Jeremiah 8:22).

This scripture actually has more than one application. On the one hand, it can be interpreted as, 'Is the blood of the lamb not in Gilead, is there no prophet there? Why then is there no recovery for Jerusalem or Israel?' On the other hand, it also refers to healing balm or medicine for the physically wounded (Jeremiah 46:11; Jeremiah 51:8). Medicine can be administered to deal with physical ailments or diseases. Taking a few pills to deal with certain conditions is not frowned upon; using some liniment or rub for a wound is not a crime. However, natural medicines are much more preferable.

"For bodily exercise profits a little" (1 Timothy 4:8).

Though bodily exercise doesn't do much for the human spirit, it can help to keep the body in shape. Exercise can be good for keeping the blood in your body moving, help fight certain diseases and conditions, improve your mood, boost your energy levels, promote better sleep, help control weight in addition to serving as a fun social activity.

"Along the bank of the river, on this side and that, will grow all kinds of trees used for food; their leaves will not wither, and their fruit will not fail. They will bear fruit every month, because their water flows from the sanctuary. Their fruit will be for food, and their leaves for medicine" (Ezekiel 47.12).

Fruits and vegetables, whilst serving as food can also help to improve the health of the body. They increase your fiber intake, provide the body with nutrients, vitamins and minerals and may help reduce the risk of certain diseases. Certain leaves and herbs can also help to treat certain conditions. Some notable ones include noni and moringa.

"Then Isaiah said, 'Take a lump of figs.' So they took and laid it on the boil, and he recovered" (2 Kings 20:7).

Chapter 6: Atmosphere for healing

Your faith is the channel for healing.

When you want to watch a particular TV channel, let's say Discovery Channel for example, your TV will tune to a certain frequency in order to receive the TV signals being transmitted from the satellite. A similar process is involved with the radio - when you want to listen to a particular radio channel, you would tune it to a certain frequency like 107.5 megahertz. When this channel is reached, the radio transmitter or satellite would send radio signals to the receiver such as the table-top radio in your home. Now you would be able to hear music or any other radio program with your receiver.

A similar thing occurs in the spiritual realm. Human beings are primarily spirits, who have souls and bodies (1 Thessalonians 5.23). The spirit is your true self, which contains the conscience and intuition, making you God-conscious and enabling you to fellowship with God. The soul contains your mind, will and emotions and is the realm of self-consciousness. The body is the outermost part of you and is responsible for your world consciousness through your five senses. Faith is a spiritual attribute that can be exercised through your spirit. Some people refer to faith as a currency that enables a believer to appropriate Heavenly blessings. Faith, working through your spirit creates a channel that connects you to God and to Heaven to receive from Him, just as a TV channel receives signals from a satellite to broadcast on the television. Usually, God gives us faith because every good thing comes from Him (James 1.17). Even the faith that got you saved to become a Christian comes from Him (Ephesians 2.8, Romans 12.3, Hebrews 12.2). Faith enables us to receive from Heaven. When faith is not exercised, it becomes difficult to receive from Heaven, "but let him ask in faith, nothing wavering. For he that wavereth is like a wave of the sea driven with the wind and tossed. For let not that man think that he shall receive any thing of the Lord. A double-minded man is unstable in all his ways" (James 1:6-8). God wants us to be steadfast in our faith so we can appropriate the many blessings He has for us. Jesus was unable to do any miracles in his hometown because they were so familiar with Him that they could not exercise the faith to receive supernaturally from Him (Matthew 13.58).

Peter was doing fine walking on the water but when He began to doubt, he began to sink; "but when he saw the wind boisterous, he was afraid; and beginning to sink, he cried, saying, Lord, save me. And immediately Jesus stretched forth his hand, and caught him, and said unto him, O thou of little faith, wherefore didst thou doubt?" (Matthew 14:30-31). God wants us to have faith in spite of our circumstances. Sometimes we are surrounded by tough circumstances that tempt us to give up, but this should not be the case. Peter saw that the wind was boisterous and that created fear in him. At that point he began to sink. Jesus then confronted Him about his doubt. This happens to us many times in life, when tough situations and circumstances create fear and panic in us when we are supposed to react with calmness. In another situation, the disciples were in a boat with Jesus. They were met with a storm at sea while Jesus was asleep. The disciples were stricken with fear and were in a panic based on the tumultuous situation at sea. The panic-stricken disciples woke Jesus up. Promptly, Jesus rebuked the storm. "And there was a calm. And he said unto them, where is your faith?" (Luke 8:24-25). Jesus did not expect them to be panic-stricken since He was with them in the boat. In contrast, Daniel's 3 friends exercised strong faith in God when they refused to bow to the idol of Nebuchadnezzar and when they were thrown into the fiery furnace. They came out without a scratch because there was a fourth man (Jesus Christ) in the fire. Faith is one of the most powerful spiritual forces in the universe. "For whatsoever is born of God overcometh the world: and this is the victory that overcometh the world, even our faith. Who is he that overcometh the world, but he that believeth that Jesus is the Son of God?" (1 John 5:4-5). Faith in Christ helps to overcome all kinds of challenges in life. Faith enables you to surmount all kinds of challenges and tough circumstances. Jesus Himself also said, "if ye have faith as a grain of mustard seed, ye shall say unto this mountain, remove hence to yonder place; and it shall remove; and nothing shall be impossible unto you" (Matthew 17:20).

One way in which faith can be expressed is through prayer. In fact, all prayer must be prayers of faith. The Bible even urges us that when we are praying, we should believe that we will receive what we are praying for and we will have them (Mark 11.24). Also, when we pray in the Holy Ghost, we build up our faith (Jude 20). Prayer and faith are intrinsically linked. Jesus' earthly ministry involved much prayer. Desiring to instill this practice in His followers He said, "men ought always to pray, and not to faint" (Luke 18:1). Prayer arrives to the throne of God as sweet-smelling incense. Prayer is power. When we pray for healing, we can have the confidence that God will answer because He has provided healing for us as part of His Covenant, so when you are praying to be healed, you can remind God that He has made provision for your healing in His Word. Paul urges the believer to "rejoice always, pray without ceasing, in everything give thanks; for this is the will of God in Christ Jesus for you" (1 Thessalonians 5:16–18). In James' epistle, he shows that prayer should be our first reaction to sickness (James 5.13-14). He also advises that when a congregant is sick, he can call for the elders to come to meet them to pray a prayer of faith to bring about healing (James 5.14). If a sick person goes to church, in the same way, he can get the elders to pray for him. The word 'elders' could be interchanged for 'pastors,' 'assisting pastors,' 'lay elders,' 'deacons,' 'visiting committee,' and so forth. When the prayer of faith is offered, James teaches that, "the prayer of faith shall save the sick, and the Lord shall raise him up" (James 5:15). It is the Lord, who does the healing; the human is only the conduit through which His healing power is manifested. James also teaches us, saying, "pray one for another, that ye may be healed" (James 5:16). If there is a Christian brother or sister you trust, you can pray or intercede for healing for each other. "Again I say to you that if two of you agree on earth concerning anything that they ask, it will be done for them by My Father in heaven" (Matthew 18:19). Furthermore, sick persons can pray for themselves; "is any among you afflicted? let him pray" (James 5:13). Do not underestimate this because healings can and do occur when people pray for themselves. Finally, James teaches that confessing our faults to one another can also facilitate healing. "Confess your faults one to another, and pray one for another, that ye may be healed" (Jam 5:16). Again, you can find a Christian brother or sister you trust for this purpose. The faults could be offences or some other kind of faults. If a trusted Christian brother or sister cannot be found, you can confess your faults to the Lord for healing. Praying for the sick must be done in faith. "And the prayer of faith shall save the sick, and the Lord shall raise him up; and if he has committed sins, they shall be forgiven him" (James 5:15).

What is faith? The Bible gives us a very accurate definition of faith because the Bible is good at explaining itself. The Bible defines faith as, "the substance of things hoped for, the evidence of things not seen" (Hebrews 11:1). The Greek word for faith is 'pistis' which can be defined as 'belief, confidence, trust, conviction.' It points to an assurance in God and in what He has said. Faith operates outside the normal 5 senses that man perceives with. Faith is from His inward man - His spirit. Though with his natural eyes, the Christian has not seen what has been promised Him, he can believe in his heart through faith that He will receive what Has been promised. In Numbers 13 and 14, the Israelites were supposed to go and spy out a Promised Land that God had promised to give them in the days of Abraham. 12 spies were sent out to the land and 10 came back with a bad report, saying there were giants on the land and that they would not be able to go in and take it. Their negative report stirred up fear in the rest of the Israelites in the camp. There were 2 of the 12, however, named Joshua and Caleb, who believed that they could go forward and take the land. Their courage served them well because when they went forward in faith, God helped them to subdue cities much greater than themselves. Those that lacked faith and had brought the negative report as well as those who feared in the camp due to the negative report all died in the wilderness eventually, without seeing the Promise Land. The writer of Hebrews comments on this when he says, "but with whom was he grieved forty years? Was it not with them that had sinned, whose carcasses fell in the wilderness? And to whom sware he that they should not enter into his rest, but to them that believed not? So we see that they could not enter in because of unbelief. Let us therefore fear, lest, a promise being left us of entering into his rest, any of you should seem to come short of it. For unto us was the gospel preached, as well as unto them: but the word preached did not profit them, not being mixed with faith in them that heard it. For we which have believed do enter into rest" (Hebrews 3:17-19, Hebrews 4.1-3).

Faith is one of the key things that pleases God. Like previously mentioned, it creates a channel of communication between the believer and God. Gifts and blessings from Heaven including healing are able to pass through this channel from Heaven to the believer. "But without faith it is impossible to please him: for he that cometh to God must believe that He is, and that he is a rewarder of them that diligently seek him" (Hebrews 11:6). We must seek God in faith and know that He would reward those who do so. It is our belief as well as our faith that enables us to see the glory of God (John 11.40). Sometimes God allows us to go through certain circumstances that try our faith. Such situations help our faith to grow stronger. "That the trial of your faith, being much more precious than of gold that perisheth, though it be tried with fire, might be found unto praise and honour and glory at the appearing of Jesus Christ: Whom having not seen, ye love; in whom, though now ye see him not, yet believing, ye rejoice with joy unspeakable and full of glory" (1 Peter 1:7-8). Our walk with God is a walk of faith (Galatians 3.11). Faith is a spiritual weapon and is referred to as a shield in the Bible. It enables the believer to overcome the devices of the enemy (Ephesians 6.16). Faith is also a strong spiritual weapon that enables the believer to appropriate the promises of God. When your faith is strong, you would stand upon the Promises of God and would subsequently take steps to appropriate those promises, believing God is a Covenant-keeping God. "Who through faith subdued kingdoms, wrought righteousness, obtained promises, stopped the mouths of lions" (Hebrews 11:33).

There are also many different levels of faith. The Bible speaks about weak faith (Romans 4.19), little faith (Matthew 16:8), strong faith (Romans 4.20), growing faith (2nd Thessalonians 1.3) and increased faith (2nd Corinthians 10.15). The Bible also talks about being rich in faith (James 2.5). Moreover, Paul spoke about visiting the church in Thessalonica to perfect their faith (1 Thessalonians 3.10). He also talks about how people who put away a good conscience and faith can find themselves in a 'shipwreck' (1 Timothy 1:19). Jesus knew how precious faith was and how much the devil wanted to take away the faith of His followers. "And the Lord said, Simon, Simon, behold, Satan hath desired to have you, that he may sift you as wheat: But I have prayed for thee, that thy faith fail not: and when thou art converted, strengthen thy brethren" (Luke 22:31-32). When the apostles needed people to support them in the ministry, so they could focus more on the Word and prayer, they looked for people who were full of faith such as Stephen and Phillip (Acts 6.5). The Bible also often speaks of steadfast faith. The Word 'steadfast' can be defined as resolute, firm, unwavering, sure, reliable and constant. We must exercise steadfast faith in our service to God and in our appropriation of His many promises, blessings and gifts (Colossians 2.5, 1 Peter 5.9, Colossians 1.23, James 1.6-8). Faith is also one of the nine fruit of the Spirit, which the Holy Spirit wishes to produce in all Christians (Galatians 5.22). Faith and love are also deeply connected. In fact, the Bible teaches that faith works by love (Galatians 5.6) and faith and love are linked (1 Thessalonians 3.7, 1 Thessalonians 5.8, 1 Timothy 1.5, 1 Timothy 1.14, Philemon 5). Having all the faith in the world without love doesn't do much because the character of God Himself is love. "And though I have all faith, so that I could remove mountains, and have not charity, I am nothing" (1st Corinthians 13:2). The Bible also considers the need for deliverance "from unreasonable and wicked men: for all men have not faith" (2 Thessalonians 3:2). In case we find out that we are lacking in faith, we can ask God to help our unbelief like the father of the sick child who said, "help thou mine unbelief" (Mark 9:24), or we can also ask the Lord to increase our faith like the apostles did, "and the apostles said unto the Lord, increase our faith" (Luke 17:5).

God is faithful, but it also takes faith on our part in order to appropriate His numerous promises. It is not surprising that Jesus told His disciples, "have faith in God" (Mark 11:22). It is essential to hold on to the precious promises of God concerning healing for you. When Jesus saw the faith of the paralytic, as well as the people carrying him on his bed and going up to the roof in order to lower him down, Jesus forgave and healed the man's sins because of his faith. It was the faith of the paralytic and his entourage that made them break through outward hindrances and external obstacles to receive healing. When blind Bartimaeus was following Jesus and seeking his healing, Jesus told him to go and that his faith had made him whole. When he was seeking his healing initially, the people around were telling him to keep quiet, but his faith made him break through hindrances set up by his fellow men and this persistence eventually made him receive his healing. When the woman with the issue of blood touched the hem of His garment, she was expressing her bold faith. She was bold enough to violate the Mosaic law (Leviticus 15) which forbade people from touching others with blood discharges. Though she was ceremonially unclean, she forsook the law and appealed to the grace of Christ. She should have been stoned for this if caught but she elbowed her way through the crowd when Jesus was moving at a fast pace to attend to the daughter of the ruler of the synagogue who was almost dead. The woman was not slow but was able to catch up. There was a throng of people surrounding Jesus, so why did He only refer to the touch of this woman? Though there were many people around Jesus at the time, she found her way through all of them to touch Him - she was able to touch Christ with her faith and this touch of faith brought her healing. The word 'touch' appears in this passage five times showing its importance. 5 is also the number of grace - the touch of the woman drew healing from the grace in Christ. She had become the star of the moment and every other activity ceased until her issue was resolved.

 Though there were many impediments, her bold faith surpassed them all to touch just the hem of Jesus' garment to receive her healing. She was so sure she would receive her healing. As a result, she didn't just say, 'if I touch the hem of His garment, I would hopefully receive some ease.' She said, "if I may but touch his garment, I shall be whole" (Matthew 9:21). She had the blessed assurance that her healing would surely ensue and it was due to a touch of faith; she had been healed immediately she touched Him. Her faith had touched the love of Jesus and He told her, "daughter, be of good comfort; thy faith hath made thee whole" (Matthew 9:22). The news of her special touch of faith must have spread because the Scriptures tell us in Mark 6.56 that, "whithersoever He entered, into villages, or cities, or country, they laid the sick in the streets, and besought him that they might touch if it were but the border of his garment: and as many as touched him were made whole" (Mark 6:56). After this healing, Jesus went to the house of the ruler of the synagogue because his daughter was nearly dead. When the people were panic-stricken, Jesus encouraged them saying, "fear not: believe only, and she shall be made whole" (Luke 8:50).

There is also much to learn about faith from the centurion whose servant was taken ill. A unique attribute of this centurion was that he was benevolent since he had compassion for his servant or yet still, his slave. He had also shown his benevolence in building a synagogue for the Jews. Moreover, he was seen as one who loved the Jewish nation and though he had not converted to Judaism, he still esteemed it. The centurion was also marked with deep humility; though the elders saw him as worthy of receiving favour from Christ, he saw himself as unworthy for Christ to come to his house. But our main focus in this section is the faith of the centurion which brought forth the healing of his servant. His strong faith is revealed when He said, "therefore I did not even think myself worthy to come to You. But say the word, and my servant will be healed" (Luke 7:7). By this, the man also showed his respect for authority. "When Jesus heard these things, he marvelled at him, and turned him about, and said unto the people that followed him, I say unto you, I have not found so great faith, no, not in Israel. And they that were sent, returning to the house, found the servant whole that had been sick" (Luke 7:9-10). He believed that just a Word of healing spoken by Jesus was enough to bring about the healing of his daughter. This man's faith made Jesus marvel!

In the case of the Syrophoenician woman, it seemed healing was not going to be her portion because first and foremost she was a Gentile. Secondly, she was considered to be a 'dog' that was not supposed to be favoured with the bread of the children. This did not stop her in any way. When she commented that even dogs eat the crumbs from the master's table, Jesus was astonished and said, "o woman, great is thy faith: be it unto thee even as thou wilt. And her daughter was made whole from that very hour" (Matthew 15:28). The fact that Jesus had delayed her healing did not mean He wasn't going to grant it. As she pressed on, it was given. Whilst Blind Bartimaeus broke through hindrances opposed by his fellow men, the Syrophoenician woman broke through hindrances of Christ Himself. Her faith had created a pipeline through which rivers of living water and healing water could flow. Jesus is always looking out for faith. In the Bible, we see verses such as, "when Jesus saw their faith" (Mark 2:5), "and when he saw their faith" (Luke 5:20), "which when Jesus perceived, he said unto them, O ye of little faith" (Matthew 16:8). Paul the apostle also looked out for the faith of the persons so that the Holy Ghost could produce a miracle for them. "The same heard Paul speak: who steadfastly beholding him, and perceiving that he had faith to be healed" (Acts 14:9). Jesus is looking out for your faith - "nevertheless when the Son of man cometh, shall he find faith on the earth?" (Luke 18:8). Now it should be said that it is not the faith that heals us - it is Christ. The faith is the channel through which we receive the blessing. When David needed water, "three mighty men brake through the host of the Philistines, and drew water out of the well of Bethlehem" (2 Samuel 23:16). In spite of opposition, you can press on till you could draw living waters from the wells of salvation. Such is the mighty force of faith.

Obedience and Healing

God wants us to obey His Word. When we obey the Word, we please God and He is able to release more blessings onto us. Jesus Himself was a good model of someone who was obedient. "Though he were a Son, yet learned he obedience by the things which He suffered" (Hebrews 5:8). Furthermore, we can learn much about obedience by looking at the experience of Naaman the Leper. Firstly, it should be noted that Naaman was a Gentile and not a Jew. When Naaman ended up in front of Elisha's abode, he was expecting the prophet to come out and meet him. The prophet didn't come out but sent a messenger to tell him to wash in the dirty Jordan 7 times. Naaman almost gave up on seeking his healing but his servants advised him to follow the directions he had been given. By following the directions, he would be debased in washing in the dirty water because he was the king of Syria. Moreover, he thought there were much cleaner rivers in Syria to wash in rather than this muddy Jordan. When he finally did, he received his healing. He almost lost his healing but humble obedience caused him to receive the blessing. In a similar way, when the Israelites murmured and God sent serpents to bite them in the wilderness, Moses prayed to God. The instruction he received was to put a bronze serpent on a pole and all who looked at it would be healed. Those who followed this instruction received their healing from the snake-bite and consequently, their venomous wounds were cured. On one occasion, Jesus healed with spittle and clay and the obedient recipient of the direction got his healing. Considering the man with the withered hand too, Jesus asked him to stretch it out. When this was done, healing resulted. On another occasion, Jesus told a paralyzed person to take up his bed and walk and when he did this, healing resulted. Sometimes, certain conditions come about as a result of not taking good care of our bodies. Resorting to better habits, remembering that the body is the Temple of the Holy Spirit will bring a change in the situation for the better. Difficulties in this area such as addictions and the like can be helped with good Christian counseling and prayer.

Another atmosphere for healing is a spiritual mindset as well as a good mental attitude. Paul often preached about a renewal of mind (Romans 12.2, Ephesians 4.23) which is very necessary after we are born-again and have become new creations (2nd Corinthians 5.17). Renewal of mind refers to studying and meditating upon the Word of God so that we become spiritually minded because our thoughts and minds are based on the Word of God; "and receive with meekness the engrafted word, which is able to save your souls" (James 1:21). The soul has 3 main compartments; the mind, the will and the emotions. This scripture ,therefore, teaches that feeding on the Word of God would set our minds aright. David also pointed this out when He said, "he restoreth my soul" (Psalm 23:3). Through the Word of God, the Holy Spirit can transform our minds for the better. A better mind would result in better health. "Finally, brethren, whatsoever things are true, whatsoever things are honest, whatsoever things are just, whatsoever things are pure, whatsoever things are lovely, whatsoever things are of good report; if there be any virtue, and if there be any praise, think on these things" (Philippians 4:8). God works through your belief system. Keep confessing your healing because the words that you speak are spirit and life (John 6.63).

Chapter 7: Now that you have received your healing

Now that you have received your healing, it is essential that you continue to use the Scriptures to secure and keep it. You had faith in the Scriptures to bring your healing about in the first place – now exercise the faith in the Scriptures to keep it. This final section of the book would help to enlighten you of how the Word of God can be used to keep the healing you have received.

"For ye are bought with a price: therefore, glorify God in your body, and in your spirit, which are God's" (1 Corinthians 6:20).

Christ purchased us with His precious blood. His blood is the lifeline for every death in our souls (Leviticus 17.11) as well as our bodies (Isaiah 53.4-5). It was a very expensive bill that was paid on our behalf by Christ on the cross of Calvary. In fact, that precious blood was shed from the foundation of the world (Revelation 13.8); the shedding of blood on Calvary was the climatic demonstration to all humanity of what had already occurred from the foundation of the world. God loves us and wants us to present our bodies and our spirits - in fact, all our being, to Him so that they will be well kept (1 Corinthians 6.20). Paul further urges us to present our bodies to God when He says, "I beseech you therefore, brethren, by the mercies of God, that ye present your bodies a living sacrifice, holy, acceptable unto God, which is your reasonable service" (Romans 12:1). If this is done, He is able to keep our bodies from a further onslaught of the devil and his demons, wishing to afflict our bodies with disease. The Bible teaches us this - "when the unclean spirit is gone out of a man, he walketh through dry places, seeking rest; and finding none, he saith, I will return unto my house whence I came out. And when he cometh, he findeth it swept and garnished. Then goeth he, and taketh to him seven other spirits more wicked than himself; and they enter in, and dwell there: and the last state of that man is worse than the first" (Luke 11.24-26).

When a spirit of infirmity is cast out of a person and he doesn't run to Christ to be safe and to be kept in the secret place of the Most High and under His shadow (Psalm 91.1) and so that the Lord would be His refuge and His fortress (Psalm 91.2), he puts himself in a vulnerable position. This opens him up for even more unclean and wicked spirits to return to him, as the void has not been replaced with Christ since those spirits left. It is essential that we look to Christ and endeavor to grow and mature in our walk with Him. The Bible further teaches us that our bodies are the Temples for the Holy Spirit to dwell in. "Know ye not that your body is the temple of the Holy Ghost which is in you, which ye have of God, and ye are not your own?" (1 Corinthians 6.19). Once we know that our bodies are the dwelling places of the Holy Ghost, we can ask God to take over our bodies as well, presenting them to Him for safekeeping because He cares about every aspect of our wellbeing. Meditating on Scriptures such as 1st Corinthians 6.19-20 and Romans 12.1 can help us in this regard.

Psalm 100.4 teaches us to "enter into His gates with thanksgiving, and into his courts with praise: be thankful unto him, and bless His name" (Psalm 100:4). It is advisable, when we want to enter God's presence, to enter with thanksgiving and praise since thanksgiving ushers us into His gates and praise ushers us farther from the gates into his courts. When we give thanks it means we appreciate God and His finished work on the cross. In fact, it is His finished work on the cross which should cause us to always give thanks, because He endured much suffering before going to it and more suffering still as He hang on it to be the sacrificial lamb for the sins of mankind. "And whatsoever ye do in word or deed, do all in the name of the Lord Jesus, giving thanks to God and the Father by him" (Colossians 3:17). Paul understood the importance of thanksgiving. He knew that He had been the chief of sinners (1 Timothy 1.15) and also knew that he had been saved and delivered by the wonderful and immense grace of God. He knew that the church God had given him was a blessing and he loved them and thanked God for their welfare and faith. "Wherefore I also, after I heard of your faith in the Lord Jesus, and love unto all the saints, cease not to give thanks for you" (Ephesians 1:15-16).

Now that you have been healed, a good place to begin would be to give God thanks and praise. It is important that you remember the condition in which you were in, when you were suffering, rejected and in anguish because of your condition. Now that healing has come, you have to be grateful to the Lord for your healing. When Jesus had healed the 10 lepers, to the surprise of Jesus, only one came back and rendered thanks. "And Jesus answering said, were there not ten cleansed? But where are the nine?" (Luke 17:17). When that leper came back and gave the glory to Jesus and thanked Him, in addition to the healing, He received a further blessing - "and he said unto him, arise, go thy way: thy faith hath made thee whole" (Luke 17:19). At first he had received healing for his body but now through Christ's abundant grace, he had received healing for body, soul and spirit. "For all things are for your sakes, that the abundant grace might through the thanksgiving of many redound to the glory of God" (2 Corinthians 4:15). It is also important that after your healing, you testify about what the good Lord has done for you. When such a testimony is given, it helps to overcome the devil because he is opposed to Jesus and His wonderful works (Revelation 12.11, 1 John 3.8). When we testify about the good works of Christ, it also helps to win more people to Him because He wants everyone to be saved and come to know him. "And through the hands of the apostles many signs and wonders were done among the people…………and believers were increasingly added to the Lord, multitudes of both men and women" (Acts 5:12,14).

 The Lord is good and He has so much in Him to offer us, including healing. When we tell others about the good He has done for us and about our healing, He does even more for us and blesses us more. "Then Jesus answering said unto them, go your way, and tell John what things ye have seen and heard; how that the blind see, the lame walk, the lepers are cleansed, the deaf hear, the dead are raised, to the poor the gospel is preached" (Luke 7:22). It is a good practice to testify of the Lord and His marvelous works. "I will praise thee, O LORD, with my whole heart; I will shew forth all thy marvellous works" (Psalm 9:1). The Lord implores us not to be worried but to offer prayers and supplications with thanksgiving (Philippians 4.6). The Lord is full of goodness and wonderful works and for these, it is right to give him thanks (Psalm 107.8). Thanksgiving should be offered not just for His goodness and wonderful works, but also because of His mercy which endures forever (Psalm 106.1, 1 Chronicles 16.34). "In everything give thanks: for this is the will of God in Christ Jesus concerning you" (1 Thessalonians 5:18).

It is also very important to give God glory for what He does for us. The Greek word for glory is 'doxa.' The Strong's concordance defines glory as, 'praise, honor, renown.' Webster's dictionary also defines it as, 'that quality in a person or thing which secures general praise or honor; that which brings or gives renown.' When God does something for us such as healing us, we need to give the glory to Him for the wonderful thing that He has done for us because, "every good gift and every perfect gift is from above, and cometh down from the Father" (James 1:17). When Jesus performed healings during His ministry on earth, many of the people gave the glory to Him (Matthew 9.8). We are to do the same. "Insomuch that the multitude wondered, when they saw the dumb to speak, the maimed to be whole, the lame to walk, and the blind to see: and they glorified the God of Israel" (Matthew 15:31). When the paralytic received his healing, he took up his bed and walked out and all the people were amazed and said they had never seen anything like that miracle, making them glorify God in effect (Mark 2.12). When Jesus was teaching in the Synagogues in Galilee, His teachings were much appreciated and as a result, He was glorified by all (Luke 15). When He rose up the dead son of the widow of Nain, all the people around were astonished and gave glory to Him (Luke 7.16). When the woman who had the spirit of infirmity that kept her body in a bent positon was healed, "immediately she was made straight, and glorified God" (Luke 13:13). When Jesus healed the ten lepers, one of them returned to Him and glorified Him (Luke 17.15). When the centurion's servant was healed, He was very grateful and glorified God (Luke 23.47). When Lazarus of Bethany became sick and the women went to report this to Jesus, He answered, "this sickness is not unto death, but for the glory of God, that the Son of God might be glorified thereby" (John 11:4). Jesus is good, kind, merciful, forgiving, loving and for these things, we need to give Him glory. "And Jesus answered them, saying, the hour is come, that the Son of man should be glorified" (John 12:23). Even Jesus Himself did all the things He did so that His Father in Heaven would be glorified (John 14.13, John 17.4, John 13.31, John 12.28). Every miracle should point to Christ Himself and God in Heaven (Psalm 115.1, Acts 3.12).

"And call upon me in the day of trouble: I will deliver thee, and thou shalt glorify me" (Psalm 50:15).

Now that healing has come, we can do certain things we could not do before. When the man with the withered hand was healed, he now had hands for service; he could now serve the Lord. "And he saith unto the man which had the withered hand, stand forth.........he saith unto the man, stretch forth thine hand. And he stretched it out: and his hand was restored" (Mark 3:3,5). The man had to take a step of faith, stand for the gospel (1st Corinthians 15.1) and also had to stretch out his hands for Christian service. When the blind man who could not see was given sight, now He could see Christ and could follow and serve Him. "They say unto him, Lord, that our eyes may be opened. So Jesus had compassion on them, and touched their eyes: and immediately their eyes received sight and they followed him" (Matthew 20:33-34). When the woman with the issue of blood received healing, she could now live life more happily, more comfortably and could have peace and stillness in her soul. "Daughter, be of good comfort: thy faith hath made thee whole; go in peace" (Luke 8:48). When the woman with the spirit of infirmity that kept her in a bent position preventing her from straightening herself was healed, now she could stand up for the Christ and His Gospel. When the lepers were cleansed, they had been freed from the bondage of sin and their consciences had been cleared; now they could be spirit-conscious. After the paralytic got healed, he was freed from his bed of affliction and could rise up (Isaiah 60.1), stand (1st Corinthians 16.13) and walk (2nd Corinthians 5.7); he could arise and shine, stand for Christ and embark on the walk of faith, such as the man Paul healed in Lystra (Acts 14.10).

Some people also like to show appreciation for healing by giving to the ministry, but this is solely due to your own discretion and free will and cannot be forced. "And certain women, which had been healed of evil spirits and infirmities, Mary called Magdalene, out of whom went seven devils, and Joanna the wife of Chuza

Herod's steward, and Susanna, and many others, which ministered unto him of their substance" (Luke 8:2-3).

Practising good and healthy habits can help to sustain your healing. The benefits of fruits and vegetables cannot be overemphasized. Moreover, eating good and healthy foods can help to maintain general health. Exercising can also help to keep your body in shape. Again, keeping a good mental attitude can help to ward off stress. Counselors have found out that having a positive mental attitude can help with your health while negative thought patterns which arise from worry, anger, fear, unforgiveness, strife, suspicion can lead to different kinds of illnesses. Sometimes, listening to some good Christian music can help to instill some peace within you in troubling times. Saul's servants spoke to him saying, "seek out a man, who is a cunning player on an harp: and it shall come to pass, when the evil spirit from God is upon thee, that he shall play with his hand, and thou shalt be well............ and it came to pass, when the evil spirit from God was upon Saul, that David took an harp, and played with his hand: so Saul was refreshed, and was well, and the evil spirit departed from him" (1 Samuel 16:16,23). But above all, it is necessary to be spiritually-minded because the Spirit of God can overcome every natural circumstance. "To be spiritually minded is life and peace" (Romans 8:6). Healing is for you; receive your healing from Christ, now!

This book was written to help aid the Christian to know of and to appropriate the healing graces of Christ for Himself so he may live in health. However, it is up to the Christian to refer to the Scriptures for Himself to know more about God's ability to heal. Always apply Acts 17.11. God bless you.

References

Hagin, K. (1997). *Laying on of Hands*. Broken Arrow, Oklahoma: Faith Library Publications.

Eckhardt, J. (2010). *Prayers that bring healing*. Lake Mary, Florida: Charisma House.

Murray, A. (1982). D*ivine Healing*. New Kensington, Pennsylvania: Whitaker House.

Prince, D. (2007). *Gifts of the Spirit*. New Kensington, Pennsylvania: Whitaker House.

Sumrall, L. (2005). *The Gifts and Ministries of the Holy Spirit*. New Kensington, Pennsylvania: Whitaker House.

Nee, W. (1968). *The Spiritual Man*. Bon Air, Virginia: Christian Fellowship Publishers.

Bosworth, F. (2008). *Christ the Healer*. Ada Michigan: Chosen Books.

Hayford, J & Cleave N.V (1997). *God's way to Wholeness*. Nashville, Tennessee: Thomas Nelson.

Hagin, K. (1993). *Seven Things You Should Know About Divine Healing*. Broken Arrow, Oklahoma: Faith Library Publications.

("Miracles and healing," 2005). Retrieved from http://healingandrevival.com/BioORoberts.htm

("Healer and Prophet," 2004). Retrieved from

http://healingandrevival.com/BioWBranham.htm

("Apostle of Faith," 2004). Retrieved from

http://healingandrevival.com/BioSWigglesworth.htm

("Leaves of healing," 2004). Retrieved from

http://healingandrevival.com/BioJADowie.htm